THEMATIC UNIT

Geology

Written by Kathee Gosnell

Teacher Created Materials, Inc.
6421 Industry Way
Westminster, CA 92683
www.teachercreated.com
ISBN-1-55734-240-7
©*1994 Teacher Created Materials, Inc.*
Reprinted, 2003
Made in U.S.A.

Illustrations by
Barb Lorseyedi

Edited by
Karen J. Goldfluss

Cover Art by
Blanca Apodaca LaBounty

Table of Contents

Introduction 3

The Magic School Bus Inside the Earth by Joanna Cole (Scholastic, Inc., 1987) 5
(Also available from Scholastic, Canada; Kingfisher Books, UK; Ashton Scholastic Pty. Ltd., Australia)

   Summary — Sample Plan — Overview of Activities — Design Ms. Frizzle's Clothes — Sequencing the Magic School Bus Journey — Is It So? — "Inside the Earth" Game — From the Ceiling - From the Ground

Wonderworks of Nature—Volcanoes: Fire From Below by Jenny Wood
   (Gareth Stevens, 1991) 17
(Also available from Saunders, Canada; Hodder Headline, Australia)

   Summary — Sample Plan — Overview of Activities — Eruptions! — Scientific Journal Magazine Article — Volcano Facts — Venn Diagram — Model Volcanoes

Eyewitness Books: Rocks & Minerals by Dr. R. F. Symes and the staff of the Natural History Museum, London (Alfred A. Knopf, 1988). 25
(Also available from Stoddart Publishing, Canada; Dorling Kindersley Ltd, UK; Harper Collins, Australia)

   Summary — Sample Plan — Overview of Activities — Rock Cycle Match-Up — Find Sherlock Homes —Crystal Gardens — Homemade Geodes

Brighty of the Grand Canyon by Marguerite Henry (Scholastic, Inc., 1967) 32
(Also available from Macmillan, Canada, United Kingdom, and Australia)

   Summary — Sample Plan — Overview of Activities — Geographical Features — Grand Canyon Rock Strata — How Did It Happen? — Experiment Form — Grand Canyon Map

Daily Writing Activities 41
Writer's Notebook — Daily Writing Topics — Create Your Own Books — Word Bank

Across the Curriculum 51

   Language Arts: Crossword Puzzle — Volcanic Word Search — Fear Factors — Mythology — Rock Specimen Report — I'm a Real Gem!

   Math: Geology Facts — Mohs Math — Plot the Answers

   Science: Magnetic Field — Exploring the Field — Rock Collections — Exploration Safety Rules — Rock Exploration Guidelines —Metamorphic Match

   Social Studies: Rocks on Your Block — Locating Geological Features — Legends in Your Own Mind — Geological Time Periods — Rocks Tell Tales - How Old Is It?

   Art: Rock Star Band — Build a Castle — Montage — "Grand" Sand Paintings

   Life Skills: Geology Careers — Campfire Cooking

Culminating Activity 76
Geology Exhibition

Unit Management 77
Bulletin Board Ideas — Achievement Award — Clip Art

Answer Key 79

Bibliography 80

Introduction

Geology contains a captivating, whole language, thematic unit about the study of geology as it relates to our understanding of the past and our hopes in using this knowledge in the present for balancing the ecosystem in the future. Its 80 exciting pages are filled with a wide variety of lesson ideas and reproducible pages designed for use with intermediate children. At its core, this literature-based thematic unit has four high-quality children's literature selections: *The Magic School Bus Inside the Earth, Wonderworks of Nature—Volcanoes: Fire From Below, Eyewitness Books: Rocks & Minerals,* and *Brighty of the Grand Canyon.* For each of these books, activities are included which set the stage for reading, encourage the enjoyment of the book, and extend the concepts gained. In addition, the theme is connected to the curriculum with activities in language arts, math, science, social studies, art, and life skills. Many of these activities encourage cooperative learning. Suggestions for bulletin board and unit management tools are additional time savers for the busy teacher. Highlighting this complete teacher resource is a culminating activity: Geology Exhibition. This activity allows students to synthesize and apply their knowledge beyond the classroom.

This thematic unit includes:

- ❏ **literature selections**—summaries of four children's books with related lessons (complete with reproducible pages) that cross the curriculum

- ❏ **writing ideas**—daily suggestions, including Big Books, for writing across the curriculum

- ❏ **group projects**—to foster cooperative learning

- ❏ **bulletin board ideas**—suggestions and plans for student-created and/or interactive bulletin boards

- ❏ **planning guides**—suggestions for sequencing lessons each day of the unit

- ❏ **curriculum connections**—in language arts, math, science, social studies, art, and life skills such as cooking and careers

- ❏ **culminating activities**—to help students synthesize their learning

- ❏ **a bibliography**—suggestions for additional books on the theme

> To keep this valuable resource intact so it can be used year after year, you may wish to punch holes in the pages and store them in a three-ring binder.

Introduction *(cont.)*

Why Whole Language?

A whole language approach involves children using all modes of communication: reading, writing, listening, observing, illustrating, and speaking. Communication skills are integrated into lessons which emphasize the whole of language rather than isolating its parts. A child reads, writes (spelling appropriately for his/her level), speaks, listens, and thinks in response to a literature experience introduced by the teacher. In this way, language skills grow naturally, stimulated by involvement and interest in the topic at hand.

Why Thematic Planning?

One useful tool for implementing an integrated, whole language program is thematic planning. By choosing a theme with corresponding literature selections for a unit of study, a teacher can plan activities throughout the day that lead to a cohesive, in-depth study of the topic. Students practice and apply their skills in meaningful contexts. Consequently, they tend to learn and retain more. Both teachers and students are freed from a day that is broken into unrelated segments of isolated drill and practice.

Why Cooperative Learning?

In addition to academic skills and content, students need to learn social skills. No longer can this area of development be taken for granted. Students must learn to work cooperatively in groups in order to function well in modern society. Group activities should be a regular part of school life, and teachers should consciously include social objectives as well as academic objectives in their planning. The teacher should clarify and monitor the qualities of good group interaction just as he/she would clarify and monitor the academic goals of a project.

Why Big Books?

An excellent cooperative, whole language activity is the production of Big Books. Groups of students or the entire class can apply their language skills and content knowledge to create additions to the classroom library. These books make excellent culminating projects for sharing beyond the classroom with parents and friends. This thematic unit includes directions for making Big Books in your classroom.

The Magic School Bus Inside the Earth

by Joanna Cole

Summary

For those who really like science, a visit to Ms. Frizzle's class would be quite a treat. Although her clothes may be a bit eccentric, her hands-on teaching methods make learning a delight, even for Arnold, one of Ms. Frizzle's unenthusiastic students.

When her students have trouble understanding or completing a homework assignment (this time, bringing a rock for earth science), Ms. Frizzle decides that a field trip is necessary. With the aid of a magic school bus, the class begins a journey to the center of the earth and back again. During their journey, they find out how soil is made, learn about fossils, rock layers, limestone caves, the mantle, the earth's core, and volcanoes. The trip is a bit unusual, but the students learn some fascinating facts about rocks and return with a great rock collection.

The outline below is a suggested plan for using the various activities that are presented in this unit. You should adapt these ideas to fit your own classroom situation.

Sample Plan

Day 1

- Read the first half of *The Magic School Bus Inside the Earth*.
- Design Ms. Frizzle's clothes (page 9).
- Build a Rock Star Band (page 73).
- Introduce magnetic fields (pages 60-61).

Day 2

- Read second half of *The Magic School Bus Inside the Earth*.
- Sequence the journey of the Magic School Bus (page 10).
- Solve Geology Facts (page 57).

Day 3

- Introduce Daily Writing Topics for *The Magic School Bus Inside the Earth*. (page 42).

- Analyze statements relating to the book (page 11).
- Learn about scientists in the field (pages 62 and 74).

Day 4

- Continue daily writing (page 42).
- Play the "Inside the Earth" Game (pages 12-14).
- Investigate Rocks on Your Block (page 67).

Day 5

- Continue daily writing (page 42).
- Build a rock castle (page 73).
- Discuss and create stalactites and stalagmites (pages 15-16).

Overview of Activities

Setting the Stage

1. Prepare your classroom for a unit on geology. Collect books, magazines, and pamphlets on geology, earth science, geologists, scientists, volcanoes, glaciers, earthquakes, rocks, and minerals. (See Word Bank listings on page 50 and the Bibliography on page 80 for ideas.)

2. Introduce the Writer's Notebook (page 41). Emphasize "clue words" which will help trigger a string of ideas. Discuss the importance of taking just enough notes to understand the information a week later. Read information from a pamphlet or encyclopedia to the class and have the students practice taking notes. Have them write only one word or phrase in their Writer's Notebook.

3. Brainstorm with the students to see how much they know about geology. Put a web on the chalkboard and let the children share their ideas about geology while you write them down. After they are done brainstorming, have them copy the web into their Writer's Notebook (page 41). When the thematic unit is completed, have students do this exercise again so they may compare and contrast what they have learned.

4. Introduce the writing topics for *The Magic School Bus Inside the Earth* (page 42). Allow students time each day to use their Writer's Notebooks to respond to one of the topics.

Enjoying the Book

1. After reading the first half of *The Magic School Bus Inside the Earth,* discuss Ms. Frizzle's classroom as it appears on the first two pages of the book. Ask students how they think their own classroom might look at the conclusion of a unit on geology. Students will enjoy the activity on page 9 as they design clothes for Ms. Frizzle that could be added to her wardrobe.

2. Have students perform the magnetic field experiment on pages 60 and 61. As students write about their experiment on page 61, encourage them to record both failures and successes with the magnetic fields. Discuss why making predictions, recording observations, and drawing conclusions are important learning tools.

Overview of Activities *(cont.)*

3. Read and discuss the remainder of the book. Emphasize the author's technique for creating imaginary happenings along with presenting geology facts. Ask students to think of other stories they have read in which a similar method was used. Go over the new Earth Science words and their pronunciations that appear at the end of the selection. Ask students if they can guess what lesson Ms. Frizzle will teach next. Discuss other Magic School Bus stories.

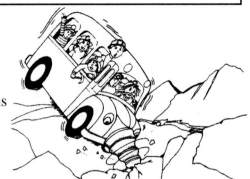

4. Ask students to sequence the events on page 10 as they review the story. Discuss their responses and ask students to add information from the book that relates to each event.

5. Have students complete the activity, "Is It So?" on page 11. After they have determined which statements are true and which are false, ask students to correct the false statements by finding the corresponding correct statements in the book.

6. Work with groups of students to construct the "Inside the Earth" Game (pages 12-14). Discuss the playing rules and allow students to play the game during appropriate time periods. **Note:** You can adapt this game to include new questions by deleting the questions on the game board and substituting them with revised material. Provide a new answer key, too.

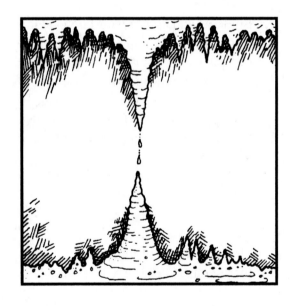

7. Have students research to find out more about caves. Plan a trip, if possible, to a nearby cave. Review the experiences of Ms. Frizzle's class as the students toured the caves. Discuss the formation of stalagmites and stalactites and the word clues that help us identify each. Have students complete the experiment on page 15 and the writing activity on page 16.

8. Solve the mathematical problems in Geology Facts (page 57).

9. Have students imagine that they were in Ms. Frizzle's class when she led her students on the geology field trip. Ask them to brainstorm other possible adventures they might have experienced on such a trip. Divide the class into small groups and have each group write its own adventure. The account should include both fictional and nonfictional details. Have groups illustrate the pages of their stories and organize them into a book. Display the completed book at the Geology Exhibition (page 76).

Overview of Activities *(cont.)*

Extending the Book

---

1. Invite local geologists into your classroom. Have them discuss their areas of expertise. Encourage them to bring rock samples, slides, or videotapes to show the class.

2. Careers in the field of geology are many and varied. Since the beginning of the Age of Computers, more opportunities have developed as new computer systems are introduced and used for analyzing much of the information that geologists gather. There are many jobs that geologists undertake. Many job opportunities also exist for other specialized branches of geology. Several are described on page 74. Encourage students to explore the various jobs available in the field of geology. After completing the activities on page 62, students can learn more by researching some of the occupations in this field and sharing their information with the class.

3. Invite a geology teacher from a local area college. Have him/her suggest how he/she would teach a unit similar to Ms. Frizzle's class visit inside the earth.

4. Have students make books using the ideas from the Word Bank (page 50) or from other materials that relate to the theme.

5. Students can add to their knowledge of geology by completing the math computations on page 57. Have students discuss their responses and the geology statements on the page. Prepare a class Big Book of geology facts complete with a decorated cover and several pages on which to record new geology facts learned throughout the unit. Begin by writing some of the facts from page 57 and continue to add to the list as unit activities and information from the literature books are discovered.

6. Provide students with a copy of Rocks on Your Block (page 67). This activity may be done as a homework assignment or as a class field trip. Have students share their completed maps and the information they gathered through extended research.

Design Ms. Frizzle's Clothes

Ms. Frizzle wore some interesting outfits. Here is your opportunity to design some new clothes for Ms. Frizzle that she might wear while teaching geology or some other subject. Don't forget shoes and a hat!

Sequencing the Magic School Bus Journey

Arrange the statements below by numbering them from 1–14 to show the order in which they happened in the story.

A. _____ Arranged and displayed rock collection.

B. _____ Collected rocks on a volcanic island.

C. _____ Dug through the earth's crust.

D. _____ Given homework assignment to bring a rock to school.

E. _____ Bus changed into a drill.

F. _____ Bus began to spin.

G. _____ Floated to school.

H. _____ Fell into a limestone cave.

I. _____ Carried along in the air from steam created by the hot lava hitting water.

J. _____ Drilled through the center of the earth.

K. _____ School bus changed into a steam shovel.

L. _____ Discovered rock layers made of sediment.

M. _____ Drove through a tunnel of black rock.

N. _____ Carried into the water by red-hot lava.

Is It So?

Much of the information that appears in this selection is true. Read each statement below. Decide whether it is true or false, according to the information in the book. Fill in the correct answer (T for true or F for false) in the boxes next to each statement.

1. Rocks are made of minerals.

2. The outside layer of the earth is called sedimentary.

3. Without rock there would be no soil.

4. Sandstone is made of grains of sand all pressed together.

5. Fossils are made of mud and clay all pressed together.

6. Shellstone is made of shells all pressed together.

7. Stalagmites are frozen icicles of water found on the floor of caves.

8. Stalactites hang from the ceilings of caves.

9. The Empire State Building is made of limestone.

10. Rocks that change from one kind to another are called igneous.

11. Rocks cannot melt.

12. The earth's inner core is made of melted rock.

13. Rocks are too heavy to float.

14. When lava cools, it hardens into new rock.

"Inside the Earth" Game

Materials: scissors; pages 13–14 (one set for each group of players); answer key and spinner materials below, reproduced on index paper (one set per group); file folders (one per game board); brad fasteners; glue or tape

Directions: Color, cut out, and glue the game board to the inside of a file folder. (You may wish to laminate the file folder for durability.) Cut out the spinner and arrow. Punch a hole in the center of each. Attach the arrow to the spinner with a brad fastener. If the arrow does not spin freely, loosen the brad a little.

Note: Reproduce the directions below, if you wish to attach them to the front of the folders.

Game Directions

This game is for 2 or more players. Use markers or small rocks as playing pieces.

1. Determine the order in which players will take turns by spinning the spinner. The player with the highest spin goes first.

2. In turn, spin to determine the number of spaces to advance on the game board.

3. Follow the directions on the game board.

4. Correct answers are provided on the answer key card and should be kept with the game.

5. The first player to get the exact number to reach FINISH wins!

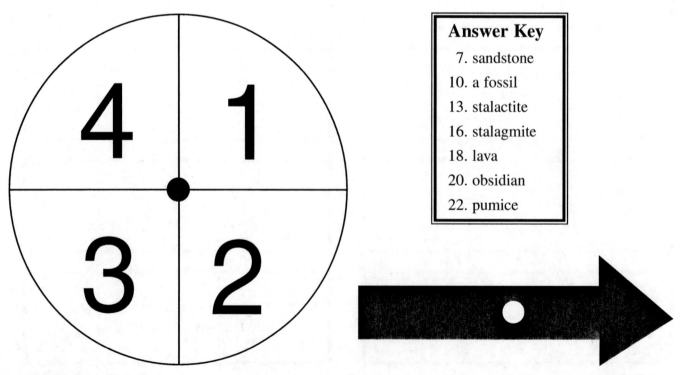

Answer Key

7. sandstone
10. a fossil
13. stalactite
16. stalagmite
18. lava
20. obsidian
22. pumice

Game

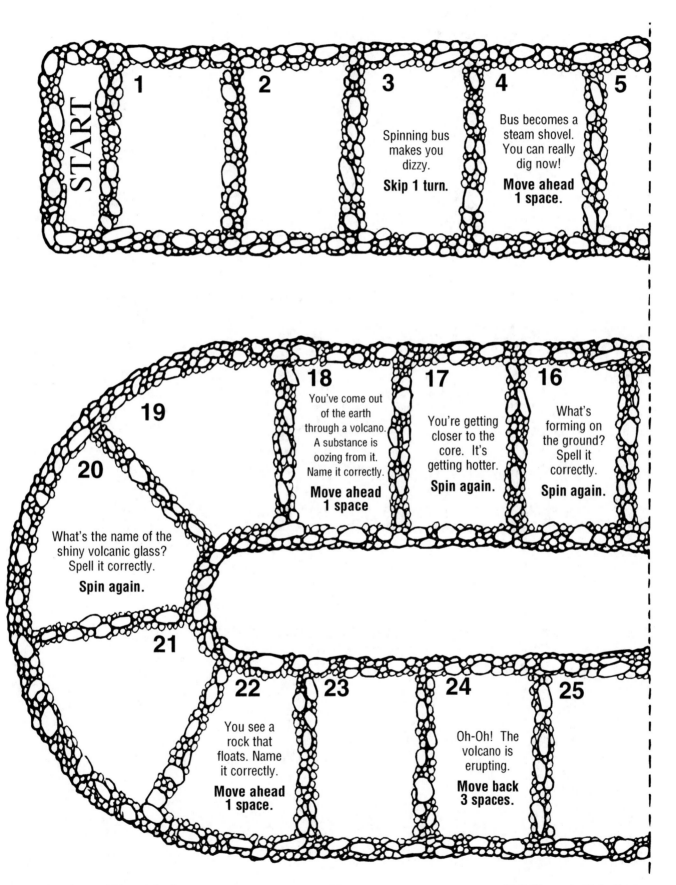

START

1

2

3
Spinning bus makes you dizzy.
Skip 1 turn.

4
Bus becomes a steam shovel. You can really dig now!
Move ahead 1 space.

5

19

18
You've come out of the earth through a volcano. A substance is oozing from it. Name it correctly.
Move ahead 1 space

17
You're getting closer to the core. It's getting hotter.
Spin again.

16
What's forming on the ground? Spell it correctly.
Spin again.

20
What's the name of the shiny volcanic glass? Spell it correctly.
Spin again.

21

22
You see a rock that floats. Name it correctly.
Move ahead 1 space.

23

24
Oh-Oh! The volcano is erupting.
Move back 3 spaces.

25

Board

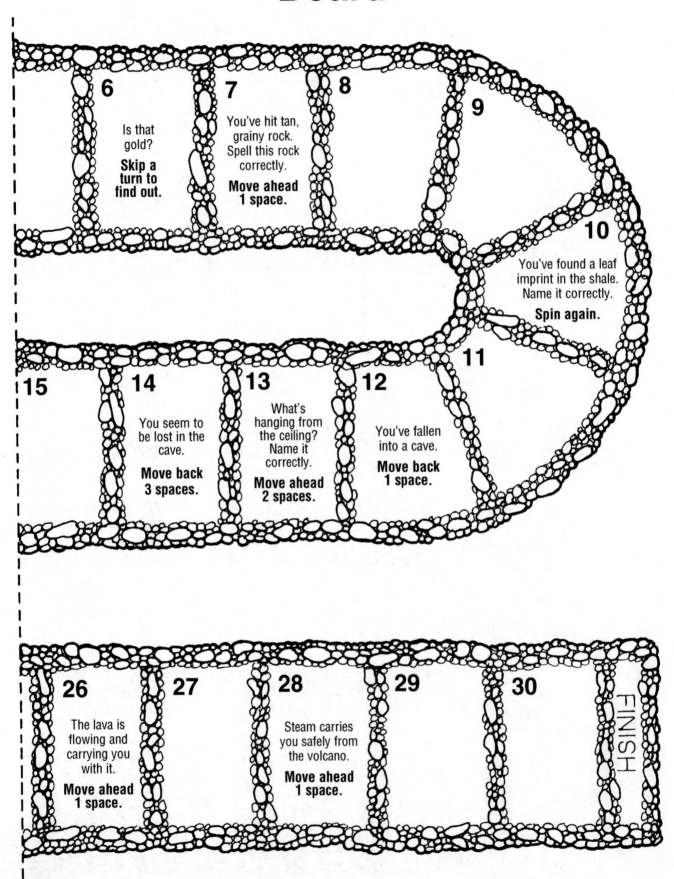

6

Is that gold?

Skip a turn to find out.

7

You've hit tan, grainy rock. Spell this rock correctly.

Move ahead 1 space.

8

9

10

You've found a leaf imprint in the shale. Name it correctly.

Spin again.

15

14

You seem to be lost in the cave.

Move back 3 spaces.

13

What's hanging from the ceiling? Name it correctly.

Move ahead 2 spaces.

12

You've fallen into a cave.

Move back 1 space.

11

26

The lava is flowing and carrying you with it.

Move ahead 1 space.

27

28

Steam carries you safely from the volcano.

Move ahead 1 space.

29

30

FINISH

14

From the Ceiling–From the Ground

Ms. Frizzle and her class discovered a cave of limestone as they journeyed inside the earth. Icicle-shaped mineral deposits (stalactites) were hanging from the ceiling and cone-shaped mineral deposits (stalagmites) had built up from the ground.

Activity

Make your own stalactites and stalagmites. Follow the directions below and observe what happens. Then, read the information about how real stalactites and stalagmites form in limestone caves.

When you have completed the activity and learned more about these formations, write a poem or paragraph on page 16 comparing stalactites and stalagmites.

Materials

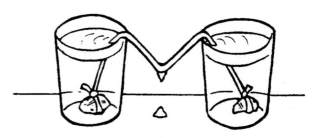

- Epsom salt or alum (available in pharmacies)
- 2 drinking glasses
- water
- soft, thick piece of cotton cord
- 2 small stones or iron washers

Directions

1. Fill both glasses with water. Dissolve as much of the Epsom salt or alum as possible in each of the two glasses of water.

2. Place the cotton cord between and into the two glasses as shown. Attach a small stone or iron washer to each end of the cord. This will prevent the cord from floating on top of the water.

3. In a day or so, observe the cord section between the glasses. You should see the formation of stalactites and stalagmites as the water dissolves, leaving the salt or alum deposits behind.

Here is what happens in limestone caves:

The limestone deposits in the water found in caves contain calcium carbonate, a chemical that gets into the limestone from sea water or from the shells of dead sea animals. Over many years, the chemical hardens into limestone.

Stalactites and stalagmites are formed by the calcium-rich water dripping from the ceiling of the cave. As the water evaporates, it leaves the calcium behind, to form stalactites. Stalagmites are built up from the ground when the water from the stalactites drips down and then evaporates.

From the Ceiling–From the Ground

(cont.)

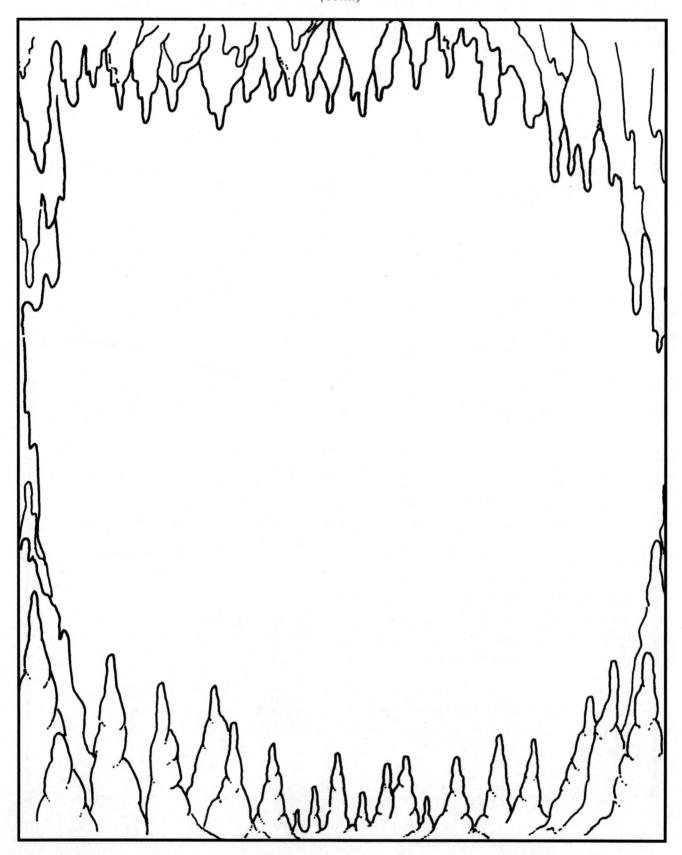

Wonderworks of Nature — Volcanoes: Fire From Below

by Jenny Wood

Summary

What is a volcano? What changes in nature occur in the area of an active volcano? Are volcanoes useful, or are they only destructive forces? These are just a few of the questions answered in this selection. Students will learn about volcanic materials, where volcanoes are found, what it is like living near a volcano, types of volcanoes, and the birth of a volcano. There is also a glossary of terms connected with volcanoes.

The outline below is a suggested plan for using the various activities that are presented in this unit. You should adapt these ideas to fit your classroom situation.

Sample Plan

Day 1

- Read pages 4-17.
- Introduce volcanic terms with a word search (page 52).
- Begin Daily Writing Topics for *Wonderworks of Nature—Volcanoes: Fire From Below* (page 42).
- Build model volcanoes (page 24).
- Research and write myths about the earth's geological features and characteristics (page 54).

Day 2

- Read pages 18-31.
- Continue daily writing (page 42).
- Discover the causes and effects of volcanic eruptions (page 20).

Day 3

- Continue daily writing (page 42).
- Write scientific journal articles (page 21).
- Discover facts about volcanoes (page 22).

Day 4

- Continue daily writing (page 42).
- Determine fear factors (page 53).
- Learn about earthquake legends and write "Legends in Your Own Mind" (pages 69-70).

Day 5

- Continue daily writing (page 42).
- Compare extrusive and intrusive rocks (page 23).
- Locate geological features (page 68).

Overview of Activities

Setting the Stage

1. Introduce the writing topics for *Wonderworks of Nature—Volcanoes: Fire From Below* (page 42). Allow students time each day to use their Writer's Notebooks to respond to one of the topics.

2. Prepare "Volcanoes Around the World" bulletin board, as suggested on page 77. This can be used as a spring board to inspire student discussion and introduction to the unit. Use the suggestions for the "Volcanoes" bulletin board on page 77. As students read and discuss the selection, and complete the activities, display exceptional papers.

3. Introduce the words from the "Volcanoes" and "Volcanic Disasters" sections of the Word Bank on page 50. Make a chart with two columns labeled "What I Think It Means" and "What It Really Means." Have students define several, or all of the volcanic terms, and write their ideas on the chart under "What I Think It Means." Ask volunteers to tell what they know about the volcanic disasters listed in the Word Bank and write their suggestions in this column also. Display the chart in a prominent place in the classroom. As the unit progresses and new information is learned, write the factual data on the chart in the column, "What It Really Means." At the end of the unit on volcanoes, have students compare the information on the chart.

Enjoying the Book

1. Read and discuss pages 4-17 in the selection.

2. Build model volcanoes using the directions and materials on page 24. Discuss "dormant" and "active" volcanoes. Discuss the geological factors that cause volcanoes. Reproduce and distribute copies of page 68 to students. Have them research individually, in groups, or as a class to find active volcanoes and related volcanic phenomena. Record the information on the map provided.

3. Have students complete the cause-effect activity on page 20. This activity is designed to help students think critically about volcanic eruptions and the effects they have had on the world. By making a visual representation, the students can more easily understand the cause and effect factors. You may wish to model the activity first. Provide a sample on an overhead projector or chalkboard. The volcanic eruption (such as Mount St. Helens) should be considered the cause. Direct students to suggest possible effects on people, on the geographical location surrounding the volcanic eruption, and on history. (Effects could include "killed 57 people," "leveled 250 square miles (650 km²) of forest," "formed fertile soils from ash and mud residues," and so on.) Record them on "lava flows" trickling down from the crater. Students can then use the diagrams to present written or oral reports on the eruptions.

Overview of Activities *(cont.)*

Enjoying the Book (cont.)

---

4. Read and discuss the remainder of the book. Discuss the dangers of living near a volcano and the birth of a volcano in Paricutin, Mexico. Discuss the impact on the people who lived in the area around the volcano. Ask students what they think would happen to them if the same thing occurred now or in their vicinity. Go over the quiz on page 29 of the selection. Review the words in the Glossary.

5. Distribute copies of page 52. Have students locate volcanic terms in the word search. Upon completion, discuss the meaning of each and add this new factual information to the chart introduced in activity 3 of "Setting the Stage" (page 18).

6. Have students make books using the directions and suggestions on pages 44-49. Display the completed books for others to read and include them in the Geology Exhibition described on page 76.

Extending the Unit

---

1. Invite students to explore the job of a volcanologist. If possible, have students interview a real volcanologist or a person who has witnessed a volcanic eruption. If this is not possible, have students use their imagination and the information they've gained. It may be necessary to have students locate information relating to volcanology and volcanologists. Distribute the journal article activity on page 21. Review the "5 W's." When students have completed the writing activity, encourage them to share their articles with the class.

2. Have students work individually or in small groups to solve the problems on page 22. As they record the answers in the statements on the page, they will discover additional facts about volcanoes.

3. Using information from the selection, materials in the classroom, school library, or other science resources, have students locate information on extrusive and intrusive rocks. Distribute copies of page 23 and ask students to complete the Venn diagram.

4. Discuss human reactions to the more violent forces of nature (volcanoes, earthquakes, hurricanes, etc.). Have students complete the exercise on Fear Factors (page 53). Share the variety of student responses and ask students to support their choices. Use the information on page 54 to explore myths about the formation of geographical features and other natural occurrences.

5. Encourage students to use their imaginations as they write their own legends. Ask them to read the legends on page 69. Together, choose one of the countries listed on the page. Locate and share information about the country's natural features, culture, climate, etc. Then, brainstorm some possible reasons for the creation of that country's legend. Have students complete the activity on page 70 and share their own legends with classmates.

Eruptions!

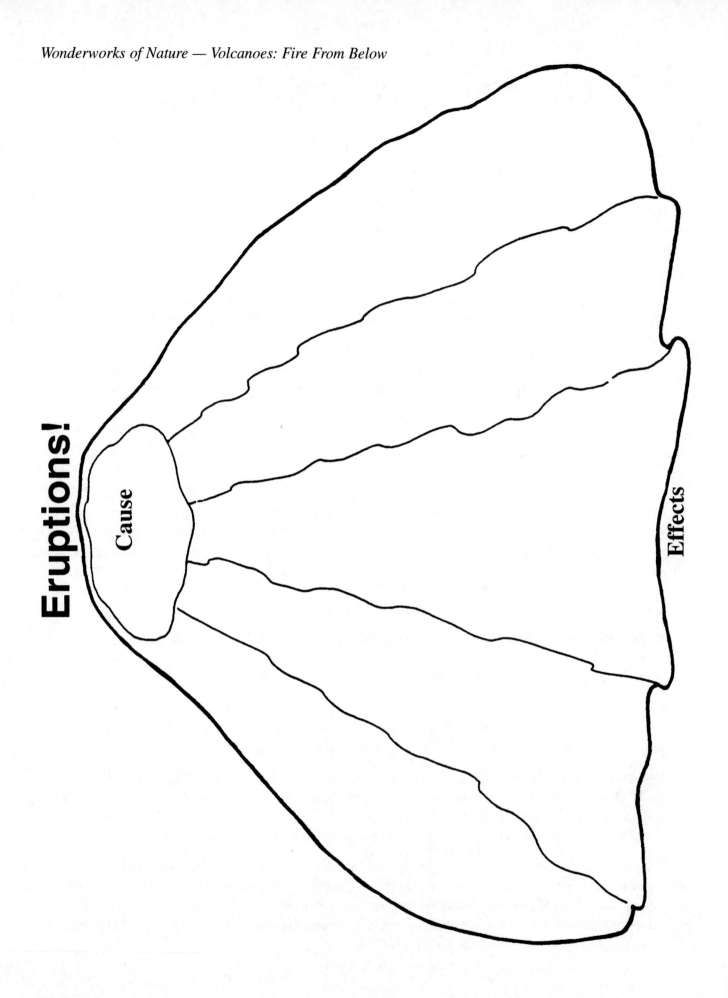

Cause

Effects

Scientific Journal Magazine Article

Pretend you are a writer for a scientific journal. It is your assignment to write a brief account of an interview with a volcanologist and the discovery of a new, active volcano. It is to be part of a feature presentation entitled: "What's Happening in The World of Geology?"

Use the 5 W's (Who?, What?, Where?, When?, and Why?) to relate the information needed in your summary. Use pre-existing volcanoes or make up one of your own. Your article does not have to be written as if it is from this time period. You may choose to go back in history or ahead into the future. Use your imagination, but remember—it is a scientific journal article, and should be accurate and brief. Create an interesting title to catch the eye of your reader.

_____

Title

Who?

What happened?

Where?

When?

Why is it noteworthy?

Extra details:

Volcano Facts

Discover some interesting facts on volcanoes as you solve the problems below. Then, on the lines above each letter in the statements, write the letter that corresponds to the answer every time you find it in the puzzle below.

A = 26 x 12 _____

E = 16 x 11 _____

I = 71 x 3 _____

M = 15 x 5 _____

Q = 39 x 4 _____

U = 62 x 3 _____

Y = 20 x 41 _____

B = 627 + 11 _____

F = 38 + 73 _____

J = 38 + 52 _____

N = 77 + 19 _____

R = 709 + 51 _____

V = 579 + 47 _____

Z = 719 + 207 _____

C = 156 ÷ 13 _____

G = 189 ÷ 9 _____

K = 104 ÷ 8 _____

O = 70 ÷ 5 _____

S = 512 ÷ 16 _____

W = 1173 ÷ 51 _____

D = 306 - 105 _____

H = 62 - 13 _____

L = 111 - 19 _____

P = 999 - 555 _____

T = 818 - 319 _____

X = 638 - 547 _____

1. A ___ ___ ___ ___ ___ ___ ___ is the huge, round crater which forms when the cone
       12 312 92 201 176 760 312
    of a live volcano collapses inward.

2. An instrument which can pinpoint the position of rising magma is called a
    ___ ___ ___ ___ ___ ___ ___ ___ ___ ___ ___ .
    32 176 213 32 75 14 75 176 499 176 760

3. A special branch of geology that specializes in the study of volcanoes, especially those that are active or might become active is called
    ___ ___ ___ ___ ___ ___ ___ ___ ___ ___ ___ .
    626 14 92 12 312 96 14 92 14 21 820

4. Volcanic ___ ___ ___ ___ ___ ___ ___ ___ ___ only began to be studied seriously
             176 760 186 444 499 213 14 96 32
    in the late nineteenth century.

5. Changes in a volcano are caused by ___ ___ ___ ___ ___ moving toward the surface to erupt.
                                        75 312 21 75 312

6. Volcanoes are also found on other ___ ___ ___ ___ ___ ___ ___ like Mars and Mercury.
                                       444 92 312 96 176 499 32

7. ___ ___ ___ ___ ___ ___ ___ ___ ___ eruptions of sticky, stiff lava commonly
    176 91 444 92 14 32 213 626 176
    produce one or more of these fragmental deposits: pyroclastic flows, ash falls, and volcanic mudflows.

8. ___ ___ ___ ___ ___ ___ ___ ___ ___ ___ ___ flows consist of glowing, hot
    444 820 760 14 12 92 312 32 499 213 12
    mixtures of pumice and ash.

9. ___ ___ ___ ___ ___ ___ ___ ___ are mixtures of fragmental, volcanic debris and
    75 186 201 111 92 14 23 32
    water.

10. A very light type of volcanic rock which can float in water is called
    ___ ___ ___ ___ ___ ___ .
    444 186 75 213 12 176

Venn Diagram

Use the information you know about igneous rocks to fill in the diagram below. In the space marked "both," write things that extrusive and intrusive rocks have in common. On the area of the cones that do not overlap, write the unique features of each.

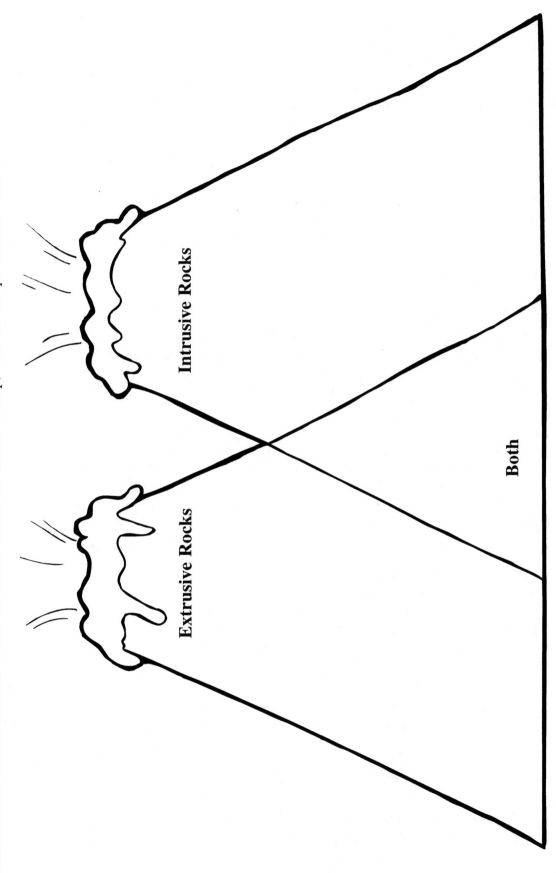

Extrusive Rocks

Intrusive Rocks

Both

Model Volcanoes

Model volcanoes are fun to build and display. They can be constructed from many types of materials found around home. Students can build erupting (live) models or dormant models using the following materials and directions. As an extension, ask students to give their model volcanoes a name and to write fictional stories or information cards about them.

Clay Model ("Dormant")

Materials: newspapers; modeling clay; dark-colored crayons; pumice; mortar and pestle; burner; 50 mL beaker; board or rigid cardboard to hold your model as a base; beaker tongs

Note: The use of the burner and handling of hot, melted crayons should be conducted by an adult using proper safety equipment.

Directions

1. Spread the newspaper over your work area. Place the base on top.

2. Have students use the modeling clay to build a mountain. A model about 6" (15 cm) high and 3" (8 cm) wide at the base would be sufficient for display. Shape it into a rugged mountainous terrain.

3. Place a 50 mL beaker over a burner and slowly melt several dark-colored crayons (with wrappers removed). Pour the melted crayon over your "volcano." This will simulate lava flow. It will harden quickly as it cools.

4. Use a mortar and pestle to grind some pumice (light volcanic rock). Leave some of the pumice in small chunks. Pour the powder over your "volcano." Push the small chunks into the sides. The result is a realistic-looking extinct volcano.

Plaster Volcano ("Live")

Give each student a marble-sized ball of clay and a cone-shaped cup. Have students put their names on the cups. Place the ball of clay inside the point of the cup. Mix plaster of Paris (about 8 pounds/3.6 kg) for a class of 30, a little bit at a time, to the consistency of thick pancake batter. Put the mix into the cups and let it set for 24 hours. Give students their volcanoes and several sheets of newspaper. Have them peel away the cup and remove the clay ball. They should have a volcano with a crater.

Stand the volcano upright on the spread-out newspaper. Prepare the volcano for an eruption. Place about one teaspoon (5 mL) of baking soda into the "crater" which has been lined with plastic wrap. Mix red and yellow food coloring with ¹/₂ teaspoon (2.5 mL) of white vinegar in a separate cup. Pour the vinegar slowly into the baking soda. Stand back and observe what happens!

Eyewitness Books: Rocks & Minerals

by Dr. R. F. Symes and the staff of the Natural History Museum, London

Summary

Eyewitness Books: Rocks & Minerals is an excellent nonfiction resource for young readers. Among the topics included in this 64 page book are: the formation of rocks; effects of erosion; exploration of igneous, sedimentary, and metamorphic rocks; crystals, gemstones, and other minerals; rock collecting; fossils; uses of rocks, past and present. Each page is filled with excellent color photographs which bring the world of rocks and minerals "up close and personal." It is suggested that this book be located in an accessible area of the classroom so that students can enjoy the wealth of information and outstanding photographs as often as possible.

The outline below is a suggested plan for using the various activities that are presented in this unit. You should adapt these ideas to fit your own classroom situation.

Sample Plan

Day 1

- Read and discuss pages 6 -16 of *Eyewitness Books: Rocks & Minerals.*
- Introduce Daily Writing Topics for *Eyewitness Books: Rocks & Minerals* (page 43).
- Match information to discover facts about the rock cycle (page 28).
- Complete a crossword puzzle to learn geology terms (page 51).

Day 2

- Read and discuss pages 17-27 .
- Continue daily writing (page 43).
- Prepare a rock specimen report (page 55).
- Match the metamorphic rocks (page 66).
- Create homemade geodes (page 31).

Day 3

- Read and discuss pages 28-42 .
- Continue daily writing (page 43).
- Use math coordinates to learn new facts (page 59).
- Create geology montages (page 73).
- Make crystal gardens (page 30).

Day 4

- Read pages 43-63.
- Continue daily writing (page 43).
- Discover gems (page 29).
- Learn about Mohs Hardness Scale by completing a math activity (page 58).
- Research and write about birthstones (page 56).
- Prepare rock collections (pages 63-65).

Overview of Activities

Setting the Stage

1. Introduce the writing topics for *Eyewitness: Rocks and Minerals* (page 43).

2. Set up a bulletin board appropriate for this section to display exceptional student papers and projects. Prior to discussion about gems, prepare a bulletin board using the "Birthstones" suggestion on page 77.

    Use the bulletin board to motivate students to learn more about these gemstones and other minerals. Assign the activity on page 56 and have students share their birthstone information with the class.

3. Introduce the words from the Word Bank on page 50 that relate to rocks and minerals.

Enjoying the Book

1. Because this selection contains extensive information in a number of areas related to the topic, you may wish to have students practice note taking and organizational skills to record important details as you proceed through the sections. One suggestion is to collect such information in the Writer's Notebook (page 41). With the class, brainstorm a set of topics and subtopics using the "Contents" page of the selection as a guide. Have students write the selected topics/subtopics in their notebooks. As you proceed through *Eyewitness Books: Rocks & Minerals,* encourage students to work individually or in groups to add information to their notebooks in the appropriate areas.

2. Reproduce and distribute page 51 to students. Use the crossword puzzle to reinforce terms used in the unit and to introduce new words for this selection. As students complete the puzzle, ask them to recall where they saw some of the terms before and to note any information they remember about them.

3. The group of minerals known as crystals is particularly fascinating to children. Crystals are grouped according to their symmetry. Discuss symmetry and note symmetrical shapes in the environment. If possible, obtain crystal specimens for students to view with a magnifying glass. Note the angles between the crystal faces. Have students create and display their own crystal gardens using the materials and directions on page 30.

    Extension: Introduce students to geodes (large, colorful crystals that form inside rocks). Distribute copies of page 31 and have students simulate geodes in the classroom.

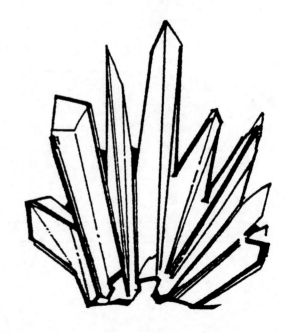

Overview of Activities *(cont.)*

Enjoying the Book (cont.)

4. After reading about metamorphic rocks in the selection, have students complete the activity on page 66. As an extension, groups of students can research other examples of rocks that were once shale or limestone. Prepare a chart with the headings "Limestone" and "Shale." On the chart, have students write and illustrate examples and descriptions of rocks for each category.

5. Read about and discuss the development and use of Mohs Hardness Scale. Have students complete the activity on page 58 to discover the hardness rating of the minerals listed.

6. Introduce students to the many varieties of gems. Have them complete the word search on page 29. Distribute page 55 to students. Assign students the task of collecting a variety of rocks and minerals in their backyards or neighborhood areas and completing rock specimen reports. Reports and rock specimens can be displayed at the Geology Exhibition.

    Note: Have students save any unused rocks they collected. The additional rocks can be used for the castle-building activity on page 73.

Extending the Book

1. Class field trips are usually a very memorable time. People take pictures and collect souvenirs to help remind them of their trip. If possible, conduct a class field trip for the purpose of collecting interesting and unusual rocks that can be sorted and used for several of the activities in the unit. Take photographs of students collecting rocks. Display the pictures and have students write captions or brief note cards about each picture.

2. Discuss the rock cycle with the class using the following example of a rock cycle and any available classroom or library sources. Encourage students to look for examples of the rock cycle as they read and explore their environment. Provide students with a rock collecting experience using the suggestions and activities on pages 63-65.

    The Rock Cycle: As magma is forced up from the mantle, it changes to lava and rolls down the sides of the volcano to the ocean where it cools, flows into the water, and changes into igneous rock. Wave action breaks the lava and igneous rock into layers of sand-sized pieces which become pressed together into sedimentary rock. Heat produced by pressure at the bottom of the sedimentary rocks causes them to change to metamorphic rocks. When this metamorphic rock is buried deeper, it gets hotter, melts, and becomes magma once again.

3. Have each student (or group of students) create a wheel book using the materials and directions on page 45.

4. Make arrangements to visit a local rock shop. Ask the proprietors to tell about running a shop. Do they get their supplies, or some of their supplies, from their own searches? Do they have a rock tumbler? Do they make or purchase jewelry? These are just a few questions you may wish to ask.

Rock Cycle Match-Up

Directions: Rocks are constantly changing. The rock cycle occurs over millions of years. Research the rock cycle. Then read the information below. On the lines before each question, write the number(s) of the line(s) which contains the answer to the questions at the bottom of the page. (Some answers may be used more than once; others not at all.)

The Rock Cycle

1. Rocks at the earth's surface are damaged by wind, rain, ice, tiny animals, and plants.

2. Some of the gases in the air, mixed with rainwater, make an acid which can dissolve certain kinds of rocks.

3. Lichens are tiny plants that make acid which can wear away the rocks on which they live.

4. Moving water can smash rocks hard enough to break them. Eventually the rocks are broken into sand.

5. Weathering is the name for the breaking up and wearing away of rocks at the earth's surface.

6. Erosion is the name for all the ways that earth materials are moved around on the surface by wind and water.

7. Sediments, bits of rock, carried by streams into lakes and oceans started to build up into thick layers.

8. Sediments pressed tightly together with the water squeezed out become sedimentary rocks.

9. Earth movements form metamorphic rocks by pressing, squeezing, and folding. Sometimes minerals are destroyed and new minerals are created.

Questions

A. _____ What is the name for the ways earth materials are moved around on the surface?

B. _____ What are sedimentary rocks made of?

C. _____ How do earth movements form metamorphic rocks?

D. _____ How can tiny plants break down rocks?

E. _____ What is weathering?

F. _____ What are sediments?

G. _____ Do minerals stay the same during metamorphosis?

H. _____ What happens to the water when sedimentary rocks are being formed?

Find Sherock Homes

Sherock Homes is missing. "Boulderdash the Rock Hound" is on his trail. Sherock left a trail to follow. It is a trail of gems. To find Sherock, you must follow the trail. The trail begins at the top with a T. Find the names of gems that Sherock put down as clues. Each gem is connected to the next word by sharing a letter, either the first letter or last letter of the next gem. One gem word is plural in the puzzle. After trailing five different gems, you will find Sherock by an A. Use the word bank below to identify the gems.

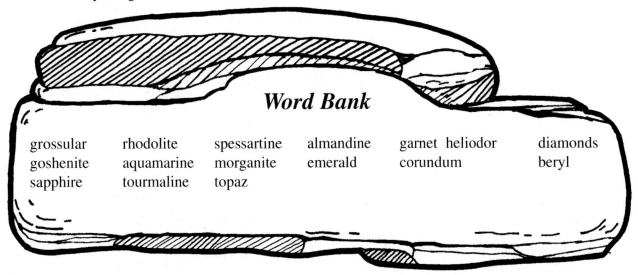

Word Bank

grossular	rhodolite	spessartine	almandine	garnet heliodor	diamonds
goshenite	aquamarine	morganite	emerald	corundum	beryl
sapphire	tourmaline	topaz			

```
L A T O P A Z C A L C T O P A Z
A X O P A K S Q N P V K E I J D
T O U R Q V B A K C G A O E T O
B A R Q E B C I R S X A L U Z T
G E M A K E N R U A S I Q F E M
A M A T A O I Q Z O X A F H A Y
R E L U Q I A I X T V U O A A N
N R I S Z Q R E Q B S X F D A A
E A N E S S Q U W H R N E T P Q
T L E M E R A L D B O S P A W U
C D I A M O N D I F L U L O R A
O I G L E N I D A P H T W C E M
R A N I R A T E M I N E R A L A
U M E N A S E E O O P I A T E R
N O O M O R G A N I T E W A S I
F A I V U A H J D A Y Q O G U N
U D S A P P H I S A P P H I R E
L S L X O U P A T Z L F Q W I A
```

Crystal Gardens

Most rocks are made up of more than one mineral.

A mineral is a substance which...

...is formed naturally in the earth's crust.

...is made up of materials that were never alive.

...has the same chemical makeup wherever it is found.

...is made up of atoms arranged in regular patterns formed into solid units called crystals.

Perhaps the most unique and attractive feature of minerals is their crystal form. Most minerals are formed in liquid and develop as crystals.

Activity

Create crystal gardens in the classroom with the following activity.

Materials: small container such as a margarine tub; piece of sponge or charcoal about the size of a golf ball; dropper bottle of food coloring; magnifying lens; household ammonia; water; salt; bluing (found in the laundry section of the grocery store or pharmacy); large glass jar for mixing; measuring cup and spoons; large spoon for stirring mixture

Directions

1. Mix the following chemical solution while students observe.

   In a large jar, mix ³/₄ cup (188 mL) each of water, bluing, and ammonia with ¹/₂ cup (118 mL) salt. (This chemical solution will be poured over charcoal and sponges to create a delicate crystal garden.) **Note:** To avoid breathing ammonia fumes, prepare the solution in either a well-ventilated area or outside.

2. Distribute the charcoal or sponge in a small container to each student or group of students.

3. Pour 2 tablespoons (30 mL) of the solution over each piece of charcoal or sponge.

4. Have students add a drop of each different food coloring in a different corner of their sponge or charcoal. Students should leave the middle without any coloring. Have students draw a picture of what they observe.

5. Leave the containers alone for 15 minutes in an undisturbed area. Have students draw what they observe.

6. At the end of the day, have students observe their containers again and draw pictures of their crystal gardens, noting any changes that may have taken place.

7. After 24 hours, have students examine their containers and draw what they see. Allow time for students to discuss and compare their crystal gardens.

Display the crystal gardens for student and parent viewing. Ask students to include written observations and/or drawings as part of the display.

Homemade Geodes

Sometimes rather large, colorful crystals form inside the cavities of rocks. Rocks containing these crystal cavities are called geodes.

Activity

Create geodes that simulate the real geodes found in nature with the following activity.

Materials: half of a coconut shell (Simulated geodes will be formed inside the shells.); a large paper cup of hot water; alum or Epsom salt (found in pharmacies); red, green, and blue food coloring in dropper bottles; spoon for stirring; magnifying lens

Directions

1. Have students work in small groups for this activity. Distribute the materials to each group.

2. Have students dissolve the alum (or Epsom salt) in the cup of hot water.

3. Add a drop of food coloring to the solution.

4. Pour enough of the solution into the coconut shell to fill it. The shells will need to sit for several days until the liquid has evaporated.

Have students write observations each day. Once the geodes have formed, ask students to discuss the simulation and compare it to the formation of naturally-formed geodes. Exhibit the geodes and crystal gardens for students and parents.

Brighty of the Grand Canyon

by Marguerite Henry

Summary

If you like adventure, mystery, stories about animals, and learning about one of the natural wonders of the world, you will enjoy our selection of *Brighty of the Grand Canyon.*

Brighty is a wild burro who is befriended by a miner (Old Timer/Hezekiah Appleyard). He also makes friends with an acquaintance of Old Timer, Uncle Jim Owen (a lion hunter). When "bad guy" Jake Irons comes into Old Timer's camp, Brighty is also there. But in time, the free-spirited burro leaves town. While Brighty is gone, a murder takes place and Jake Irons, a prime suspect, takes over Old Timer's mining operation. Many years pass as Brighty roams the Grand Canyon. He winters in the canyon and summers upon the North Rim. He even spends some years as a leader of a wild herd of burros. He runs into Jake Irons, Theodore Roosevelt, and others exploring the wonders of the Grand Canyon. Eventually Brighty is instrumental in the capture of Jake Irons.

The outline below is a suggested plan for using the various activities that are presented in this unit. You should adapt these ideas to fit your own classroom situation.

Sample Plan

Day 1

- Read from "Bright's World" through "The Fight in the Cave."
- Introduce Daily Writing Topics for *Brighty of the Grand Canyon* (page 43).
- Discover Geographical Features (page 35).
- Diagram the rock strata of the Grand Canyon (page 36).

Day 2

- Read from "Curious First Aid" through "The Battle Scars of Freedom."
- Continue daily writing (page 43).
- Simulate the formation of sandstone (page 37).

Day 3

- Read from "The Carrot Cake" through "A New World for Brighty."
- Continue daily writing (page 43).
- Simulate the formation of fossils (page 38).

- Research Geological Time Periods (page 71).
- Create sand paintings (page 73).

Day 4

- Read from "A Voice from the Past" through "Alone with the Night."
- Continue daily writing (page 43).
- Conduct an erosion experiment (pages 38-39).
- Make a time line of geological time periods (Extension, page 71).
- Explore campfire cooking (page 75).

Day 5

- Read from "Strange Thanksgiving" through "The Way Home."
- Continue daily writing (page 43).
- Plot geographical locations on a map of the Grand Canyon (page 40).
- Discover how rocks tell tales (page 72).

Overview of Activities

Setting the Stage

---

1. Introduce the writing topics for *Brighty of the Grand Canyon* (page 43).

2. Do prior knowledge idea webs about the Grand Canyon and wild burros. At a table or center in the classroom, place reference books and other resources about the Grand Canyon. If possible, display pictures and diagrams that show the strata.

3. Discuss other books that the students may have read by the same author. (See the Bibliography on page 80.)

4. Introduce the Word Bank list of terms related to the Grand Canyon on page 50.

Enjoying the Book

---

1. Read and discuss pages 7-50. Talk about the diction that Old Timer uses. Encourage your students to pronounce the words as written, such as: "li'l ole pussyfooter!", "eenamost", " 'Tain't hay!", " 'zactly", "alarum clock", etc. Have them try to figure out what is meant. Note that Uncle Jim Owens speaks the same way.

2. Read and discuss pages 51-92. Discuss historical fiction. Ask students to provide other examples of historical fiction and make comparisons. Have students read biographical information on Theodore Roosevelt to find out what he promoted because of the Grand Canyon's impact on him.

3. Conduct the erosion experiment on pages 38-39. Have the students compare and contrast the results of their experiments with what happened in the Grand Canyon.

4. Read and discuss pages 92-138. Discuss the building of the suspension bridge and its effect on the people and animals using it.

5. Read the information on page 36 about the rock strata of the Grand Canyon. Then, draw a diagram representing the layers of sedimentary rock. The walls of the Grand Canyon contain fossils of plants and animals that lived millions of years ago. Have students create their own fossils with the activity on page 38.

6. Read and discuss pages 139-182. Discuss Brighty's new world and how he became entangled with Jake Irons' life again.

7. Write the names of the geological time periods listed on page 71 on the chalkboard or a chart. Divide the class into small groups and assign each a time period to research. Ask each group to locate information about the geological conditions and the approximate time span of the period. Have groups share their information with the class. Distribute page 71 and ask students to complete the activity and extension.

8. Have students read pages 183-223 to discover how the "Moon Lily Tea" traps Jake Irons into confessing to the murder of Old Timer. (The answer is in the last section of the selection.)

Overview of Activities *(cont.)*

Enjoying the Book (cont.)

9. Write "Rocks Tell Tales" on an overhead projector, chalkboard, or large piece of paper. Ask students what they think this statement means. Distribute page 72 to students. Have them read the data and complete the activity and extension on page 72. Encourage students to locate additional facts about fossil and rock discoveries. Keep a class log of recorded findings made by the students.

Extending the Book

1. The Grand Canyon was formed as it cut through over a mile (about 2 km) of sandstone rock. Inform students that sand is actually small pieces of rock. Sandstone starts off as beach or river sand. After millions of years, minerals grow between the tiny grains and "cement" them together to form solid rock. Students can experience a simulation of the "settling" process that takes place in the formation of sandstone. Have them read about this process and complete the activity on page 37.

2. Since minerals come in lots of colors, the layers of sandstone (like those in the Grand Canyon) come in lots of colors, too. Have students make layered sandstone pictures by following the directions on page 73.

3. Many times in the story of *Brighty of the Grand Canyon*, Brighty managed to show up in someone's camp in time to eat. Cooking over an open fire is a skill that is not practiced much any more. However, students can learn about open fire cooking, and perhaps experience it, using the information and recipe for campfire beans on page 75.

4. Have students list the main characters that appear in the selection. Find a quote credited to each character. On a note card, write the quote on one side. On the other side, write the name of the character. (For example: Brighty—"Danger, mares! Bunch up! Gather in your colts!") Have students break into small groups. Ask them to take turns reading their quotes, allowing the other group members to guess the character. They could do the same thing using a sentence or two that describes the character.

5. Have students list three things they read about in the selection that they would like to learn more about. Have them list different sources where they might find the information. Decide whether they should research one or all of their listings.

6. Have students work in groups or by themselves to prepare questions and possible answers for the fictional parts of the story. There may be several possible answers to a question. Accept reasonable questions and responses.

EXAMPLE:

Q: What happens to Homer Hobbs? Does he take that job as a lumberjack at Flagstaff?

A: No, he decides to stay at home and keep working with Uncle Jim Owens.

34

Geographical Features

Some Grand Canyon features that appear in *Brighty of the Grand Canyon* are described below. Write the name of each landmark in the space provided. Use the Word Bank to help you.

1. A narrow opening caused by a crack or split: ___ ___ ___ ___ ___ ___ ___

2. A large stream of water: ___ ___ ___ ___ ___

3. Grass–covered area: ___ ___ ___ ___ ___ ___

4. Deep crack in the earth's surface: ___ ___ ___ ___ ___

5. A crack or opening: ___ ___ ___ ___

6. A small, high, flat region with steep sides: ___ ___ ___ ___

7. A long, narrow valley between high cliffs: ___ ___ ___ ___ ___ ___

8. An elevated tract of level land: ___ ___ ___ ___ ___ ___ ___

9. A small stream of water: ___ ___ ___ ___ ___

10. High, steep rock: ___ ___ ___ ___ ___

11. A wall or bank along a trail: ___ ___ ___ ___ ___ ___ ___

12. A hollow place inside the earth: ___ ___ ___ ___

13. A large rocky raised part of the earth's surface: ___ ___ ___ ___ ___ ___ ___ ___

14. A large area covered with trees: ___ ___ ___ ___ ___ ___

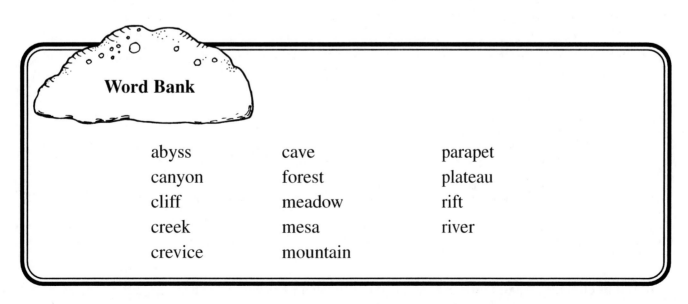

Word Bank

abyss	cave	parapet
canyon	forest	plateau
cliff	meadow	rift
creek	mesa	river
crevice	mountain	

Grand Canyon Rock Strata

A large sampling of the geological history of the earth can be seen in the rock strata of the Grand Canyon. The huge piles of rocks were created as rocks formed all over the world. The shifting of the earth's crust created them after a long, long time. As the earth's movements were building them up, a river cut down through them. These two processes, along with natural weathering and erosion, created this fantastic gorge over millions of years.

At the bottom of the canyon, under the Colorado River, are gneiss (coarse-grained, banded rocks) and granite left there by lava from volcanoes. Fossil sea creatures embedded in some of these rocks prove that an ocean once covered the area. Sediment filtered in on top of these rocks, solidified, and shifted as the earth plates moved.

The two main groups of rock at the bottom 12,000 feet (3.6 km) are called the Grand Canyon Series. They extend far below the river. The layer above these groups is called the Tonto Platform. It is 950 feet (285 m) thick. It is basically a layer of limestone and green shale. The Redwall layer is located above the Tonto Platform. It is about 500 feet (150 m) thick. It is actually blue-gray limestone that has been colored red from the red shale and sandstone from the thicker Supai layer above it. The Supai layer is 1,100 feet (330 m) thick. The next layer is 300 feet (90 m) thick. It is made of dark gray Coconino sandstone. At the top of the Grand Canyon is an 800 foot (240 m) layer of light-gray Kaibab limestone full of fossilized shells, bits of coral, sponges, and agate.

Activity

- Draw a diagram representing the Grand Canyon rock strata. *Strata* is a geological term meaning the layers of sedimentary rock representing the deposits of a single geological period.

- Use tagboard or butcher paper and draw it to scale. If you use $1/4$" (.6 cm) = 100 feet (30 m), you'll need a piece of paper 3 $1/2$ feet (105 cm) long.

- Use a color-code key to represent the different layers.

- Add brief notes about the special features of each layer. Display your diagram in the classroom.

How Did It Happen?

The Grand Canyon is one of the most spectacular canyons in the world. Some of the rocks date back two million years! Over the centuries, water and weather conditions eroded the layers of rock, which resulted in the formation of the canyon walls. The canyon walls contain fossils of plants and animals that lived in the Grand Canyon area millions of years ago. As the Grand Canyon formed, it cut through nearly 1¼ miles (2,000 m) of mainly sandstone rocks. It may be hard to imagine all these happenings on such a "grand" scale. Try the activities below and on page 38. Share what you learn from the process and results of each activity. Compare your classroom observations with what happened as the Grand Canyon was being carved out of the earth.

Settle Down!

Sandstone, as the name suggests, is rock formed from grains of sand. Over thousands of years, layers of sand settled on the bottom of the sea and became "cemented " together by chemicals in the water. Today, sandstone remains where the sea used to be.

See for yourself how small rock particles "settle down." Fill a large jar one-third full of soil. Add enough water to fill the rest of the jar. After stirring the contents well, leave the jar undisturbed for a few days. You should see the grains of different sizes settle in different layers. Complete the picture below to show the results of your "Settle Down!" experiment.

How do you think sandstone was formed in the Grand Canyon? _____

_____

_____

How Did It Happen? *(cont.)*

Creating Fossils

It takes many thousands of years for a rock to be formed. During this time, plants and animals die and decay, leaving behind fossil prints in the rock. Fossils are usually found in limestone.

Follow the directions below to make your own fossils. Pretend that you are an archeologist who discovered the fossils. Write a journal account describing where you uncovered the fossils and how you think the fossils may have gotten there.

Materials: 1 ½ pints (.7 mL) milk carton, cleaned and dried (remove top section); 1 bar modeling clay; plaster of Paris (prepared according to package directions); a choice of "fossil" items (shells, leaves, bones, etc.)

Directions: Press the modeling clay into the bottom of the carton and smooth out the top of the clay. Press the chosen "fossil item" firmly into the clay and carefully remove it. This will create an impression from which to make the fossil imprint. Pour a layer of the prepared plaster of Paris over the impression until it is completely covered. Set it aside to dry. Tear the milk carton away from the clay and plaster. Separate the plaster from the clay. You now have a fossil!

Note: This type of fossil is called a "positive fossil." To create a "negative fossil" grease the top of the positive fossil with petroleum jelly and place it in a second prepared milk carton. Pour a second layer of the plaster of Paris mixture over the positive fossil until it is completely covered. Set it aside to dry. Remove the carton and separate the fossil. Now you have two different kinds of fossils!

All Washed Up!

Erosion is caused by the moving, wearing away, or changing that takes place on the earth's surface. It creates many geological changes on earth over a period of time. You can observe soil erosion on a smaller scale with the following experiment.

Materials: 1 cup (about 250 mL) each of sand, fine soil, and small stone; water; watering can; board (about 1" x 8" x 36"/ 2.5 cm x 20 cm x 91 cm); wood block or brick; tray large enough to catch water run-off

Directions: Place the board on a block or brick so that it is on a slight incline. This will allow the water to run off at a slow to medium speed. Place a tray at the bottom end to catch the water runoff. (See diagram on page 39.) Mix the rock material together. Place rock mixture on high end of the board. Slowly pour water onto the rock mixture.

Observations: As you pour the water, notice how the materials are carried away with the water. You should see a trail of different materials clumped together on different parts of the board. Try to vary your experiments by changing the incline of the board, the speed of the water, and any other variations you wish. Fill out the Experiment Form on page 39 for each test.

Experiment Form

Name_____ Date _____

Experiment Title

In this activity, I experimented to find out _____.

I did my experiment in the following way:

_____

_____

_____

Complete the picture to show where the different soils remained on the board.

What I found out about erosion was _____

_____

What do you think this experiment reveals about the effects of erosion on the formation of the Grand Canyon?

_____

_____

Grand Canyon Map

On the map below, note the geographical locations mentioned in *Brighty of the Grand Canyon*. Use an encyclopedia or atlas to help you place the locations listed in the Word Bank.

Word Bank

Bright Angel Creek	Ribbon Falls
North Rim	Kaibab Forest
South Rim	Colorado River
Devil's Backyard	Cliff Springs
Roaring Springs	Kaibab Suspension Bridge

Draw and label an arrow on the map to show the direction that you would have to travel in order to reach each of these locations: Flagstaff, Utah, Fredonia, House Rock Valley, and Coconino County.

Writer's Notebook

A writer's notebook is a handy tool for students to keep track of their writing activities, ideas, notes, and assignments. Every student should have a notebook or a folder with his or her name and a title on the cover. The notebook is used to record ideas, take notes, and write assignments from daily writing topics and other writing activities related to the unit.

Encourage students to use their folders or notebooks to keep track of any handouts you may give them. Reproduce the cover on page 46. Have students color the page and attach it to the front of a folder or notebook. Add interior pages as needed.

How to Use the Writer's Notebook with the Unit

The notebook can be used to record written responses, notes, or whatever you and your students decide is noteworthy for all or some of the books in this unit. In this way, students will have available the information they may need for group discussion, comparing or analyzing information, and reflection. Keeping notes is a good way for students to remember information. For example, with activities that may require verbal or written feedback from *Brighty of the Grand Canyon,* students may take notes while reading each section. Here are some note-taking ideas:

1. List characters as they appear in each section. Write descriptions.
2. Note the setting, or settings, and important events of each section.
3. Note major changes that occur in characters or settings.
4. Note problems or goals that occur and/or are solved.
5. Note page and paragraph where Word Bank words are found. Define each word.

At first, taking notes while reading may slow readers down, so allow ample time to finish each reading selection. Plan to review the notes after the reading is completed, during group discussion time. This will give the students an opportunity to understand the best way to consolidate their activities and condense their information. The extra time you take in the beginning will benefit your students as they become more aware of the material they are reading. With time and practice, your students should understand what you expect of them.

Remind students to use clue words to help remember the key ideas of the text— either a whole idea or just a sentence.

In a text that has a lot of information, students can create their own glossary in the notebook to help remember the terms they are reading about. By recording these terms in their notebooks, students have an accessible resource for quick reference.

Take some time to evaluate students' workbook entries. Non-judgmental responses will please and encourage the students to write more. Remind your students that inventive spelling is acceptable while taking notes.

Daily Writing Topics

As each of the following books is read, encourage students to choose ideas from the writing topics below and on page 43. Have them write on a regular basis and share some of their written ideas.

Reproduce the word bank on page 50 to be used as a handy resource for each student. Have students keep the Word Bank in student folders or notebooks.

✏️ *The Magic School Bus Inside the Earth*

1. Pretend you are the new student in Ms. Frizzle's class. Describe your first day in her classroom in a letter to your former classmates.

2. Make a list of the students in Ms. Frizzle's classroom. Add a sentence about each of them. Use your imagination!

3. Pretend you are a fashion editor. Write an article about an interview with Ms. Frizzle. Concentrate on the unusual clothes Ms. Frizzle wears.

4. Pretend you are Arnold. Write a diary entry about being in Ms. Frizzle's class.

5. Imagine that you are a bus mechanic. Write an article about taking care of (maintaining) a magic school bus.

6. You are a spelunker who has been exploring the cave when the magic school bus crashed through the ceiling. Explain in a letter to an Alien Research Information Bureau about what you saw and heard.

7. You are an airplane pilot who has flown over the erupting volcanic island. Write a report on what you saw and the strange, colorful sight floating in the cloud of steam.

8. Imagine yourself as Ms. Frizzle. Write some lesson plans for a geology field trip.

✏️ *Wonderworks of Nature—Volcanoes: Fire From Below*

1. Write an article about what a volcano is. Use your own words.

2. Write a report on the "Ring of Fire."

3. Imagine that you are a newspaper reporter. Write a report on the birth of a volcanic island similar to Surtsey.

4. Write a pamphlet advertising a certain area containing hot springs and/or geysers for tourists. Remember that you are trying to convince them to visit these areas.

5. Write an article about what it would be like living near a volcano. If you do not actually live near one, after you have researched the assignment, add a paragraph to compare it with natural disasters, such as tornadoes, hurricanes, earthquakes, or floods that may occur in your area.

6. Pretend you are a TV news reporter. Interview a volcanologist at the site of a live volcano.

7. Imagine that you are Dionisio Pulido. Tell the tale you have told your grandchildren about the birth of a volcano in your cornfield, in the form of a diary entry.

Daily Writing Topics *(cont.)*

✏️ *Eyewitness Books: Rocks & Minerals*

1. Imagine that you have found a rock but you are not sure if it is igneous, metamorphic, or sedimentary. Write a description of the rock that would help identify the group to which it belongs.

2. Pretend that you are an archaeologist. You just discovered a stone implement used by early people. Write a journal entry that describes the tool and your thoughts about how it may have been used.

3. You have decided to take up rock collecting as a hobby. Make a list of the equipment you think you will need to be a rock collector. Next to each item, explain how you will use it.

4. People sometimes have difficulty distinguishing between stalactites and stalagmites. Write a poem or acrostic that will help others identify each.

5. Pretend that you have been on a rock hunt. You choose five rocks. Each has a color, shape, or texture that makes it unique. Now imagine that each rock creates a "mood" of its own. Give each of your "mood rocks" a name, write about the mood it generates, and explain how a person holding it might behave.

✏️ *Brighty of the Grand Canyon*

1. Imagine yourself as the Old Timer. Write a letter to your sister and little Mimi. Tell about Brighty and the new mine you have discovered.

2. Write a wanted poster for Jake Irons. Include pictures.

3. Pretend you are Joe or the red-bearded man. Write an entry in your diary that tells what happened when you tried to get Brighty to pack your cameras and stuff.

4. Write an article, as Uncle Jimmy Owen might have, that will appear in a hunting magazine. The article should be about Brighty and the fight with the big cougar in the cave.

5. Write an interview with President Roosevelt about his visits to the Grand Canyon.

6. Interview Quentin Roosevelt for a newspaper article about his first cougar hunt.

7. Write a short biography about Homer Hobbs.

8. Write a letter from Uncle Jimmy Owen to a veterinarian friend. Tell him about curing Brighty's pneumonia with his cough mixture and the hollow carrot.

9. Pretend you are a geologist that is working on the suspension bridge. Write a letter to your family, telling them about the work and the dedication.

10. Picture yourself as the sheriff. Write an account of the capture of Jake Irons. Include the confession and the "Moon Lily Tea."

Create Your Own Books

Have students make books using various suggestions throughout the unit. You can use the suggestions in the "Daily Writing Topics" (pages 42-43) or ideas introduced by students. Students writing books in groups or individually may consider a more elaborate format, such as the following one.

Parts of a Book

1. **Front Cover** — includes book title, author's name, illustration, and illustrator's name. (Example: *Birth of a Volcano* by Grade 5, Mrs. Klatt's Room.)

2. **Title Page** — includes book title, author and illustrator, and publishing company.

3. **Dedication Page** — honors one or more special people.

4. **Table of Contents** — lists what is inside the book by subject or by authors.

5. **Author Page** — describes the author. This page can include the author's family background, hobbies, and other books written by the author.

6. **Back Cover** — may include an illustration and book reviews from magazines, book clubs, newspapers, etc.

Several methods for making books are introduced below and on page 45. Select one appropriate to the book topic and purpose.

Big Books

Ready-made, blank Big Books are available at educational supply stores. If you wish to make your own, follow the directions below.

Materials: tagboard or heavy paper; metal rings; hole reinforcers; crayons; colored pencils or markers; scissors; glue

Directions

- Punch three holes on the left hand side of each sheet of tagboard or heavy paper. Cover the front and back of each hole with reinforcers.

- Have students write the text, adding illustrations where appropriate, on each page or on paper strips which can be glued to the pages.

- When all pages are completed, have students put the pages in order and make a front and back cover for the Big Book. Attach all pages with metal rings.

- Have students share their Big Books with other students or classes. Display Big Books on a large table along with projects on geology.

Create Your Own Books *(cont.)*

Shape Books

Materials: construction paper, tagboard, or heavy paper; crayons; colored pencils or markers; pencil; scissors; stapler

Directions

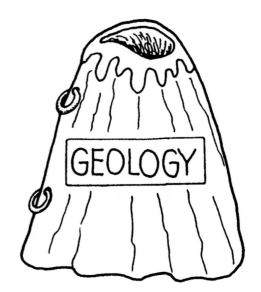

- Reproduce enough copies of the shape book pattern on page 47 to use as book pages.

- Provide each student, or group of students, with a copy of the pattern for the cover. You may wish to reproduce covers on a different color of paper. If available, use index paper to create a heavier book cover.

- Have students write the text on each page. Encourage them to include illustrations. Arrange the finished pages in order and staple them together along one edge.

Wheel Books

Materials: construction paper or tagboard; scissors; crayons or colored pencils; brad fasteners; pencil

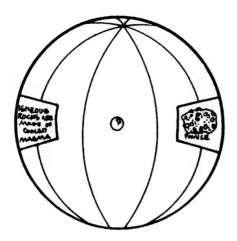

Directions

- Make copies of the patterns on pages 48 and 49. Have students cut out the wheel pattern (page 49), the earth pattern (page 48), and the dashed windows on the earth pattern (page 48).

- Help students attach the center of the wheel behind the earth with a brad fastener.

- Have students align the right-hand window on page 48 with a wheel section underneath it. Draw a picture (relating to the unit) in the section. Inside the wheel section on the left-hand window, have students write a sentence or a word describing the picture.

- To complete the wheel book, have students turn their wheels to the next blank section, draw another picture, and repeat the procedure described above until all wheel sections have been filled. (There should be six written sections and six picture sections.)

Notebook or Folder Cover

Geology

_____

(student name)

46

Shape Book Pattern

See page 45 for directions.

Wheel Book Pattern

See page 45 for directions.

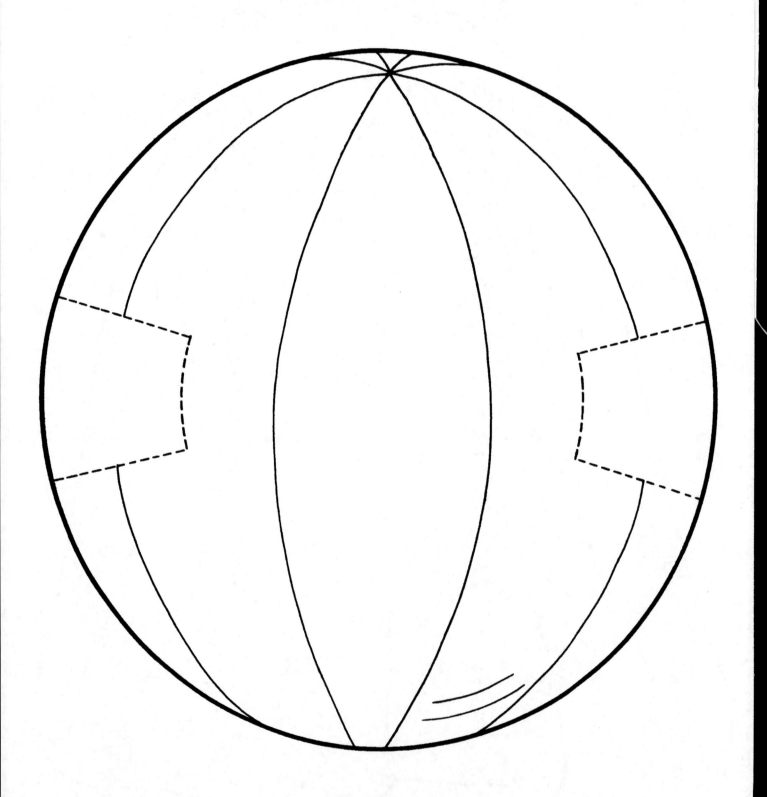

Wheel Book Pattern *(cont.)*

See page 45 for directions.

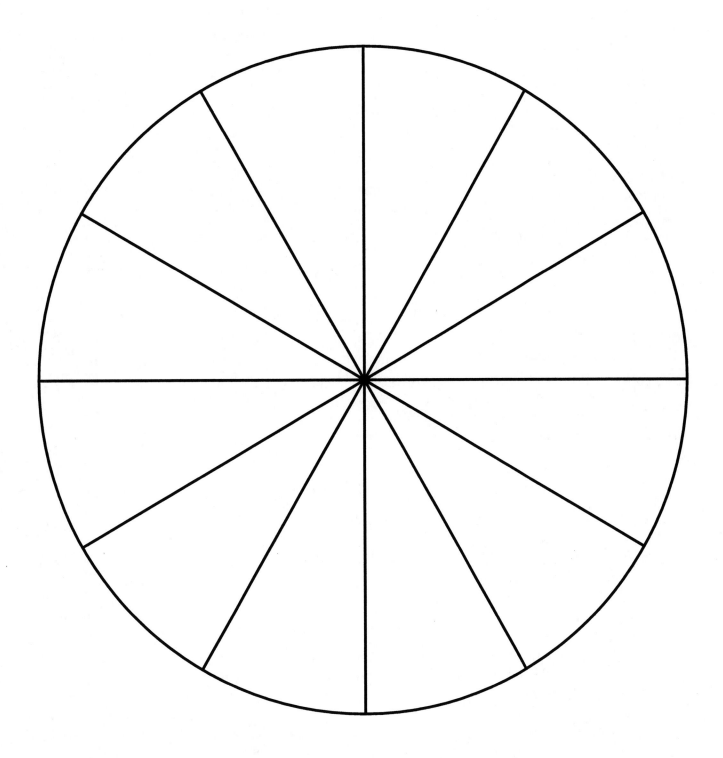

Word Bank

Volcanoes

caldera	hot spot	Ring of Fire
cone	lava	seismometer
core	magma	tiltmeter
crater	mantle	vent
crust	pahoehoe	volcanic ash
geyser	plate	volcanic bomb
hot springs	pumice	volanic plug

Volcanic Disasters

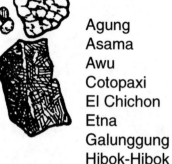

Agung	Kelut	Mount St. Helens
Asama	Kratatau	Navado del Ruiz
Awu	Laki	Oshima
Cotopaxi	Lamington	Santa Maria
El Chichon	Makian	Taal
Etna	Mayon	Tambora
Galunggung	Merapi	Unzen
Hibok-Hibok	Mont Pelee	Vesuvius

Rocks and Minerals

borates	intrusive	sedimentary
carbonates	metamorphic	sulfates
chromates	native elements	sulfides
extrusive	nitrates	sulfosalts
halides	oxides	
igneous	phosphates	

Geologists and Scientists

James D. Dana	James Hutton	Harry Fielding Reid
Clarence Dutton	Sir Charles Lyell	Charles W. Richter
Beno Gutenberg	John Milne	Adam Sedgwich
Sir James Hall	Friedrich Mohs	Emil Wiechert

Grand Canyon

Bright Angel Creek	Kaibab Forest	Ribbon Falls
Colorado River	Kaibab Suspension	Roaring Springs
Colorado Plateau	Bridge	Devil's Backyard

Crossword Puzzle

To acquaint you with names and terms that will be used throughout this thematic unit, complete the puzzle using the word bank below.

Word Bank

cone
core
crust
earthquake
erosion
fault
fossil
igneous

lava
magma
metamorphic
Mohs
plate
pumice
stalactite
stalagmite

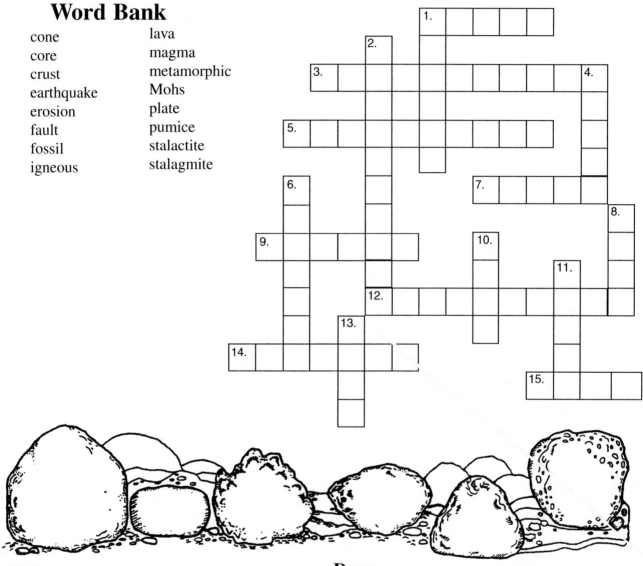

Across

1. thick slabs of rock making up the earth's crust
3. rock changed by heat and pressure
5. cave icicles formed by dripping water from ceiling
7. place where a plate of rock cracks and the two sides shift
9. a plant or animal remain from the past
12. shock waves
14. rocks made from cooled magma
15. liquid magma flowing from a volcano

Down

1. lightweight rock that floats
2. cones formed by dripping water on the ground of caves
4. earth's thin surface layer
6. wearing away of the landscape
8. innermost part of the earth
10. invented a scale to test hardness
11. molten, liquid rock far below surface
13. mountain built up around a volcano

Volcanic Word Search

Find and circle the volcanic terms from the word bank at the bottom of the page that are hidden in the puzzle below. The hidden words may appear vertically, horizontally, or diagonally.

```
T  E  I  Z  P  L  A  T  E  J  E  Y  S  R
O  P  L  Y  X  A  Z  Q  L  C  N  O  I  E
T  A  C  T  I  V  E  C  A  R  M  U  P  S
I  H  A  A  N  A  X  D  P  U  M  I  C  E
P  O  L  J  V  X  L  C  N  S  G  Y  L  I
M  E  D  K  L  E  C  R  A  T  E  R  I  S
E  H  E  Q  U  Z  N  O  O  T  Y  R  A  M
T  O  R  D  C  L  E  T  N  X  S  N  D  O
T  E  A  M  O  A  X  O  O  E  E  C  L  M
E  N  T  K  R  R  I  M  A  N  R  I  X  E
R  A  G  L  E  C  M  A  G  M  A  A  C  T
V  E  E  N  T  A  Z  A  L  A  D  F  G  E
P  L  A  N  T  Y  I  N  N  A  X  H  R
A  N  C  T  I  L  T  M  E  T  E  R  L  M
T  M  A  N  T  D  E  X  K  L  F  N  I  T
E  N  T  E  R  E  D  T  L  E  N  O  O  C
```

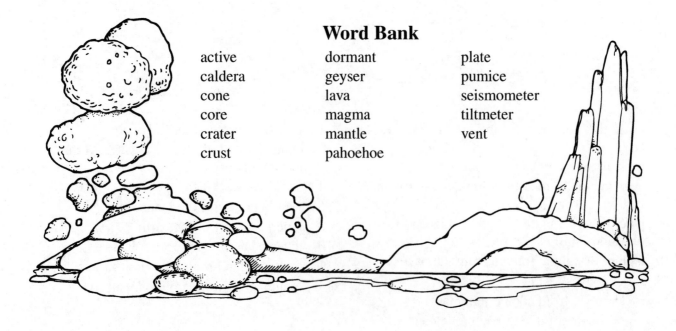

Word Bank

active   dormant   plate
caldera   geyser   pumice
cone   lava   seismometer
core   magma   tiltmeter
crater   mantle   vent
crust   pahoehoe

Fear Factors

The forces of nature have caused widespread destruction and death throughout the world and recorded time. Modern scientists have many sophisticated methods of observing, predicting, and warning us of impending disasters. But nature still manages to sneak an attack past scientific observations. Nature needs to be feared, as a manner of respect. Sometimes our fear is more that of dread or fright or terror. Sometimes our fears are unfounded. Which of these natural disasters do you fear the most? Why?

Activity

In this activity, you can rate your "fear factor" for each listed disaster. You must explain your rating by using evidence from the reading selections and/or life experiences.

Word Bank		
earthquakes	hurricanes	avalanches
volcanic explosions	flash floods	blizzards
tsunamis	tornadoes	lightning strikes

Choose one of the disasters from the word bank. Insert the word in each blank. Then, choose a number from the ratings that best fits your fear factor. Be prepared to support each rating by explaining why you chose it.

1. _____ are occurrences I fear 1   2   3   4   5 .
   little   greatly

2. _____ 1   2   3   4   5 occur near my home.
   never   often

3. The warnings for _____ are 1   2   3   4   5 adequate.
   not very   very

4. Deaths from _____ 1   2   3   4   5 occur.
   rarely   always

5. _____ are 1   2   3   4   5 dangerous compared to _____ .
   not very   very

Mythology

In ancient times, most people believed that gods and goddesses lived throughout the world. They believed the sun and moon were gods; thunder, war, love, the sea, and death (to name a few), were all gods and should be worshipped. The stories that tell about the gods and goddesses are called myths. The study of myths is known as mythology.

These myths were not just stories to tell around the hearth or campfires. Myths became part of their religion. People did not have the scientific knowledge that is available today to explain nature's ways. If a volcano erupted, it was believed to be caused by an angry or evil god.

The ancient Romans believed that there was a god of fire. According to their myths, Vulcan was that god. Vulcan was the son of Jupiter and Juno. He was also the god of the forge (for metal working). He was the blacksmith for the other gods. He made shields, breastplates, spears, and arrows. He was also considered to be the god of volcanic eruptions. Vulcans Throne is the name of a cinder cone in the Grand Canyon.

In some cultures, when volcanoes erupted, they thought the gods were angry. To stop the volcanoes from erupting again, they believed they had to give the volcano human sacrifices. That was a good reason to pray for the volcano to stop. Some people would think it an honor to be thrown into a live volcano.

Throughout history, many societies have created myths to explain the characteristics and formation of certain geographic features.

Activity

Research to find out more about myths, especially those related to the formation of the earth's features, or make up your own. What would the god of earthquakes be like? Brainstorm, as a class, some ideas about different types of gods or goddesses. Then break up in smaller groups or individually to write some myths. Put them together in a booklet. Add illustrations to make your mythology book complete.

Rock Specimen Report

Geologists become involved in many activities as they study rocks and fossils. Some do laboratory research while others explore the minerals that appear in different parts of the world.

Activity

You can be a geologist in your own backyard or neighborhood. Gather some interesting rocks in your neighborhood. Try to choose a variety of different colors, shapes, and types of rocks. Place your rocks in a sack.

Write a specimen report about one (or more) of the rocks you collected. For each rock you choose to write about, use the form below to gather your information. Share your report (and your rock) with the class.

Specimen Report

Type of Rock: _____

Rock Name: _____

Place/Date of Discovery: _____

Size and Shape: _____

Weight: _____

Coloring: _____

History of Rock (Where I think it came from): _____

_____

Discovered by _____
(your name)

Additional facts/information about my rock: _____

_____

_____

I'm a Real Gem!

Have you ever been asked, "What is your birthstone?" Birthstones are gems which signify to the month of the year in which you are born. It was once thought that a birthstone brought good luck. Today people often purchase a birthstone for a birthday gift.

Find out more about the history of the uses and beliefs related to birthstones. Locate information about your birthstone and write about it in the space below. Use descriptive language to tell about the amazing mineral crystal that represents your birth month.

Birthstone

_____

_____

_____

_____

_____

_____

_____

_____

_____

_____

_____

_____

_____

_____

Geology Facts

Discover some interesting facts about geology. Solve each problem below. Then write the answer in the blank.

1. $\begin{array}{r} 52 \\ \times\ 25 \\ \hline \end{array}$	2. $4\overline{)680}$	3. $10 \times 10 =$
4. $\begin{array}{r} 1345 \\ +\ 438 \\ \hline \end{array}$	5. $81 \div 9 =$	6. $\begin{array}{r} 756 \\ -\ 159 \\ \hline \end{array}$
7. $\begin{array}{r} 2.5 \\ \times\ 6 \\ \hline \end{array}$	8. $\begin{array}{r} 49 \\ +\ 46 \\ \hline \end{array}$	9. $\begin{array}{r} 33 \\ -\ 28 \\ \hline \end{array}$

1. Worldwide, more than _____ volcanoes have erupted at least once during the past 10,000 years.

2. A tsunami (tsoo na me) is an extremely destructive sea wave, usually triggered by large earthquakes or eruptions, and can reach heights of _____ feet.

3. Yakima, located about _____ miles downwind of a volcano, received more than an inch of ash.

4. After observing the weird weather patterns that followed the eruption at Laki Volcano in Iceland in _____ , Benjamin Franklin became the first person to figure out that volcanic eruptions could affect climate.

5. The strength of earthquakes is measured on the Richter scale, which is numbered from 1 to _____ . Most earthquakes are caused by rocks moving along faults.

6. Faults are fractures, or cracks, in rock layers along which the rocks have moved. The San Andreas fault in California, is about _____ miles long.

7. A sudden movement along the San Andreas fault in 1906 caused the destructive San Francisco earthquake. Near the city, the fault moved _____ feet.

8. In the top 10 miles of the earth's crust, _____ % of the rocks are either igneous (formed from molten magma) or metamorphic (changed by heat, pressure, or chemical action).

9. Geologists think that the age of the earth is about _____ billion years.

Mohs Math

You can test the hardness of minerals by scratching one mineral with another. A harder mineral will scratch a softer mineral. In 1822, Friedrich Mohs, a German mineralogist, used this fact to develop a scale of hardness. The Mohs Hardness Scale ranks 10 minerals from softest to hardest, with 1 representing the softest, and 10, the hardest mineral. The hardness of a mineral is established by scratching it with, or allowing it to be scratched by, the minerals on the Mohs scale.

Activity

Use your math skills to discover for yourself the ranking of the minerals on the Mohs Hardness Scale. After completing the activity below, share your responses with the class.

Directions: Determine the rank (from 1–10) of each mineral according to the Mohs Hardness Scale. First, assign each letter in each word a number from the key. Next, add up the numbers for each word to arrive at a sum. (See the example below.) Write the totals for each mineral in the hardness chart below. Use the totals to complete the rank order of each mineral on the scale below.

Example:

M	=	3
I	=	13
N	=	17
E	=	1
R	=	5
A	=	1
L	=	2
total	=	42

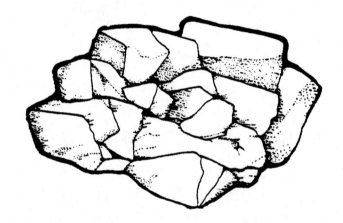

Key

A	= 1	O	= 4
C	= 2	P	= 12
D	= 7	Q	= 8
E	= 1	R	= 5
F	= 2	S	= 1
G	= 2	T	= 1
I	= 13	U	= 1
L	= 2	Y	= 2
M	= 3	Z	= 20
N	= 17		

Hardness Scale

Mineral	Total	Rank Order
diamond	_____	_____
talc	_____	_____
quartz	_____	_____
gypsum	_____	_____
fluorite	_____	_____
corundum	_____	_____
feldspar	_____	_____
calcite	_____	_____
topaz	_____	_____
apatite	_____	_____

Plot the Answers

Learn some facts about rocks and minerals as you find the missing words in the sentences. Use the number pairs listed in each sentence to determine the missing letters on the grid. Then, write the correct letter on the proper line in the sentence. **Reminder:** Use the numbers at the bottom of the grid to find the first number of the pair.

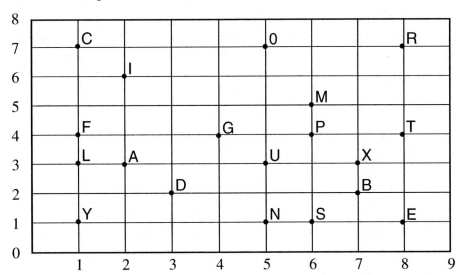

1. Sulfides are ___ ___ ___ ___ ___ ___ ___ ___ ___ that have atoms of sulfur and
   1,7 5,7 6,5 6,4 5,7 5,3 5,1 3,2 6,1
   atoms of a metal.

2. The sulfides are important because they provide important metals. Minerals that are mined for their metals are called ___ ___ ___ ___ .
   5,7 8,7 8,1 6,1

3. Pyrite is the most common sulfide mineral on earth and is found just about everywhere. Sometimes it looks like gold. Pieces in streams have fooled miners, so it was nicknamed
   ___ ___ ___ ___ ___ ,   ___ ___ ___ ___ .
   1,4 5,7 5,7 1,3 6,1   4,4 5,7 1,3 3,2

4. Sulfosalts are minerals that have sulfur, a metal (either silver, copper, or lead), and a semimetal. The semimetals are bismuth, antimony, and ___ ___ ___ ___ ___ ___ ___ .
   2,3 8,7 6,1 8,1 5,1 2,6 1,7

5. The ___ ___ ___ ___ ___ ___ are very important minerals. Oxygen is a part of the air
   5,7 7,3 2,6 3,2 8,1 6,1
   we breathe. It is also in water and magmas.

6. The ___ ___ ___ ___ ___ ___ ___ ___ ___ ___ are a group of beautiful and very
   1,7 2,3 8,7 7,2 5,7 5,1 2,3 8,4 8,1 6,1
   common minerals.

7. ___ ___ ___ ___ ___ ___ ___ ___ have a nitrogen atom surrounded by three oxygen
   5,1 2,6 8,4 8,7 2,3 8,4 8,1 6,1
   atoms. Sodium is a nitrate found in dry, desert areas.

8. ___ ___ ___ ___ ___ ___ is probably the most common sulfate. It has a Mohs
   4,4 1,1 6,4 6,1 5,3 6,5
   hardness of two, and can be scratched with your fingernail.

59

Magnetic Field

The points where the earth spins on its axis are called the North Pole and South Pole. If you could draw a line from one to the other through the center of the earth, you would find that they are exactly opposite. These two poles are actually geographic poles. There is another set of points called magnetic poles. They, too, are opposite each other and located several hundred miles from their counterparts.

You've probably experimented with compasses to see how they react to magnetism. Did you know that if you followed the direction of your compass needle across the frozen seas of the Arctic icecap, you would eventually come to a spot where the needle would swing wildly around and around, not pointing in any one direction? You would then be at the magnetic North Pole.

Scientists have decided that the earth's magnetic field is similar to a dynamo. A dynamo is a device used for converting mechanical energy into electrical energy using a conductor in motion and a surrounding magnetic field. Perhaps you've built a generator using insulated copper wire, wrapped as you would for an electromagnet, and U-shaped magnets. Setting the wire in motion within the center of the magnets produces energy. Scientists explain the earth's magnetic field with the Dynamo Theory. (A theory is an idea that has considerable evidence to back it up, but cannot be totally proved. Once it is proved, it then becomes a fact.) The Dynamo Theory says that the earth's crust and mantle (which contains metallic rocks) spin at a different speed than the inner core (which is rich in metal). This acts as a dynamo, producing an electric current in the core, and a magnetic field in and around the earth. It is as if the earth had a giant bar magnet inside it.

You can better understand the earth's magnetic field by making your own picture of it. Use the activity below to demonstrate the earth's magnetic field. Then, try the experiment on page 61. Share your findings with the class.

Materials: small bar magnet; iron filings; piece of drawing paper

Directions:

Draw a picture of the earth with its diameter about twice the length of the bar magnet. Put the magnet under the paper. Remember to point it slightly away from the geographic North and South poles. Sprinkle iron filings evenly over the paper and tap it gently. Observe the arrangement of the iron filings. Compare it with the picture on page 61.

Magnetic Field *(cont.)*

Magnetic Field Diagram

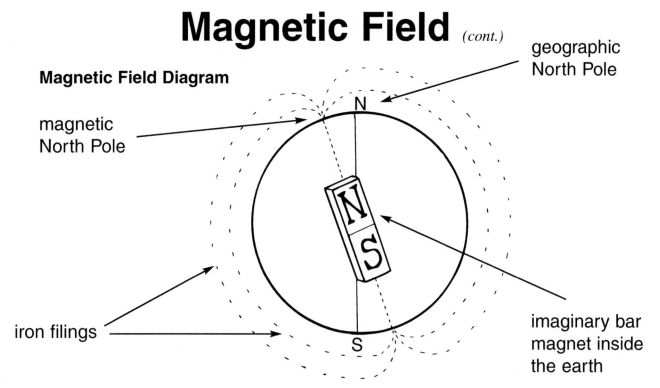

geographic
North Pole

magnetic
North Pole

iron filings

imaginary bar
magnet inside
the earth

Experiment

Use a small compass to see how it lines up with the magnetic field when placed at certain positions near your picture. In the space provided, write your predictions, observations, and the results of your experiment. (Be sure to include failures as well, should you experience any.) Share your findings with the rest of the class.

Magnetism Experiment

_____

_____

_____

_____

_____

_____

_____

Exploring the Field

A scientist asks many questions and tries to learn the answers through experimentation. Geology is the science of the earth. It includes the exploration of volcanoes, earthquakes, icecaps, deserts, underwater mountains, underground caves, rocks, and minerals.

Someone who studies geology is called a geologist. A geologist will study and offer theories about when the earth was formed, how it developed, and what the inside of the earth is like. By exploring these questions, geologists learn where to find coal, oil, water, iron ore, and useful rocks. They also learn the best places to build dams, highways, tunnels, and skyscrapers.

There are some scientists who specialize in a specific branch of geology. A volcanologist is someone who deals with volcanoes, especially those that are active or might become active. A seismologist is a scientist who studies earthquakes and the plate movements producing them. A mineralogist determines what minerals are found in certain rocks. A microscopist is an expert in determining the crystals formed from minerals. A crystallographer examines the patterns of molecules inside a crystal and deduces which elements are present and how they're combined. A paleontologist studies fossils to interpret what the earth must have been like at various periods of geologic history.

These scientists collect data (information) by observing, measuring, and carefully recording and analyzing their research. They report their failures as well as their successes. They write reports about their findings (results) so that others can learn from their experiments.

Activities

1. In the article above, locate each word listed in the word bank. Using colored pencils, underline each word with a different color. Then, with the same color for each word, underline its definition.

2. Look up the words in a science dictionary to discover how to pronounce them. Write them phonetically in your Writer's Notebook.

3. Choose one of the areas of geology that interests you most. Research to find out more about the work involved in this field and about the job of the scientist. In your Writer's Notebook, write what you consider to be the most interesting facts from your research.

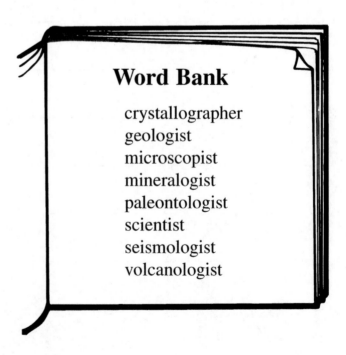

Word Bank

crystallographer
geologist
microscopist
mineralogist
paleontologist
scientist
seismologist
volcanologist

Rock Collections

Rock collecting is a hobby that people of all ages can enjoy. Families plan outings such as hiking and camping trips that include searching for rocks. The investigation of rocks and minerals helps to uncover much about the earth and its history. Collecting them teaches students to care about the planet on which we live.

When starting any new project, it helps to have an expert explain what he or she knows about the project. Invite an expert into the classroom to share his or her knowledge with the students. Major cities have mineral and gem clubs. These clubs often have activities for young collectors. Some local museums may have exhibits showing rocks, and minerals, and even fossils, that are found in the area. If so, plan an outing to acquaint yourself with what you can expect to find, and where to look.

The best places to look for rocks and minerals are quarries, cliffs, mine dumps, roads, and railways. Any rocky outcrop could prove interesting. River beds and banks, beaches, and building sites are other good places to look. Before collecting, decide together what equipment will be necessary. Here are some suggested materials:

- a strong shoulder bag or backpack
- a geological hammer (a regular hammer at one end with a pointed end on the other) specifically made for breaking rocks
- tissues, cotton, envelopes, or newspapers to wrap specimens
- a notebook to record where and when you found each rock and to describe the surrounding area
- pen or pencil
- sticky labels or adhesive tape to mark each item
- heavy gloves
- safety glasses
- guide book for identification

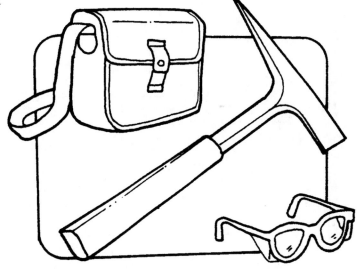

After determining where to explore, brainstorm, as a class, a set of rules for safe exploration. (e.g., If you have to hammer rocks, do so on the ground while wearing safety glasses.) Have each student copy the rules in the space provided on page 64. Students can keep a copy in their notebooks.

Students should be aware that all landscapes have potential dangers. Discussing them beforehand should minimize these dangers. Be sure to get permission to visit any sites that are on private land.

Exploration Safety Rules

1 _____

_____

2 _____

_____

3 _____

_____

4 _____

_____

5 _____

_____

6 _____

_____

7 _____

_____

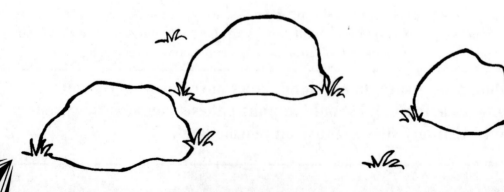

Rock Exploration Guidelines

- Use a guide book to identify any rocks or minerals that you find. Label a specimen with its name and the place where it was found. Wrap items carefully and store them in bags.

- When you return from your field trip, carefully wash specimens in warm soapy water to remove any loose dust and dirt. Some samples may dissolve in water, so be certain to test those you suspect may be destroyed in this way.

- Allow each sample to dry. Display samples in a box or a drawer that you've lined with felt or tissue paper. Hold each rock in place with glue or clay. Add a label beside each sample with its name and the other information you have gathered.

- Organize your specimens into some systematic grouping. One way to sort your collection is by rock type: igneous, metamorphic, or sedimentary. Use the information in the following chart to help you decide in which category you should place each rock specimen.

Name	Characteristics	How Formed	Usually Found
Igneous (granite, basalt, obsidian, pumice, quartz)	glossy, crystalline, coarse-grained	created when molten lava cools	where volcanoes have existed
Metamorphic (slate, schists, magmatite, marble, eclogite)	hard, crystals may appear, layers may develop	created when sedimentary or igneous rocks undergo a change due to pressure or heat within the earth	deep in the earth where pressure and heat can affect the rocks
Sedimentary (chalk, coal, sandstone, shale, limestone, dolomite)	contains fossils, soft, layered	created when layers of sediment (mud, sand, gravel, and minerals) settle to the bottom of the ocean and over thousands of years are pressed together	where oceans or bodies of water once existed or still exist

Metamorphic Match

Metamorphism means change of form. Metamorphic rocks are created by heat and pressure within the earth. Older rocks may be melted and squeezed and take on new forms. Metamorphic rocks began as one kind of rock and later, were changed into another kind. All of them began as sedimentary or igneous rocks. As the change to a metamorphic rock occurs, the structure and sometimes the color changes too. To find metamorphic rocks, you have to find an area where *weathering* (the breaking up and the wearing away of rocks at the earth's surface) and *erosion* (the moving of earth materials by wind and water) have cleared away the sedimentary rocks to expose the metamorphic rock underneath.

Activity

Below are some rocks that have been changed. (You will notice that some rock names have been repeated in Column B. This is because some metamorphic rocks began as the same rock type but underwent changes.)

Use your library or classroom resource books to find information about the origin of each rock below and how it changed. Match the changed rocks (from Column A) with the rocks they once were (from Column B). Record the words from Column B next to the correct rocks from Column A.

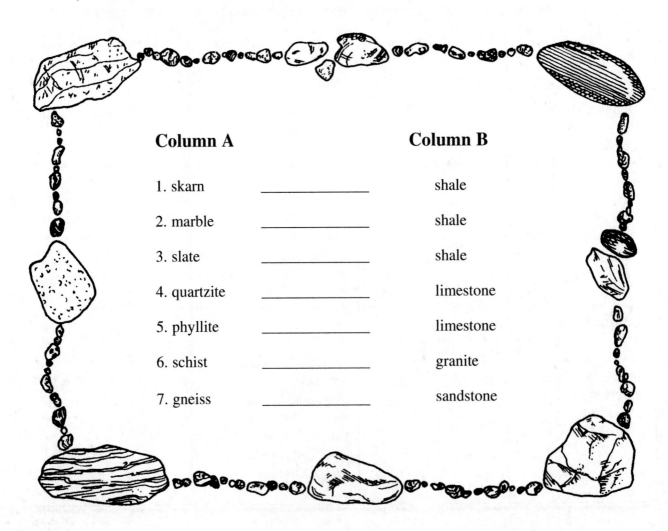

Column A

1. skarn _____

2. marble _____

3. slate _____

4. quartzite _____

5. phyllite _____

6. schist _____

7. gneiss _____

Column B

shale

shale

shale

limestone

limestone

granite

sandstone

Rocks on Your Block

Everywhere you go you are standing on rocks. Even the soil in your yard is made of ground-up bits of rock. Some rocks occur naturally, while others are used for building and decorating. How are rocks used in your neighborhood? Are rock materials used in the homes, buildings, monuments, landscape decorations, fences, etc.?

Activity

Find out how rocks are used in your immediate neighborhood, at your school, or in other areas of your community. In the box below, make a simple map to show the area you have chosen to survey, and indicate the various uses of rocks in that area. Include a key to explain your information.

Extensions: Research to find out how the rocks got to the area. Are they from a nearby quarry? Do they appear as field stones brought by glaciers? Were they shipped from other locations? Write reports to display with your maps.

Locating Geological Features

Volcanoes usually form where two plates collide and one is forced to slide beneath the other as, for example, in the so-called "Ring of Fire" around the Pacific Ocean. Other volcanoes are formed by hot spots, areas of fierce heat in the mantle which cause magma to bubble up toward the surface. On the map below, locate live volcanoes and other related information such as hot spots, plate edges, and the "Ring of Fire." Include a key for locating the information on your map.

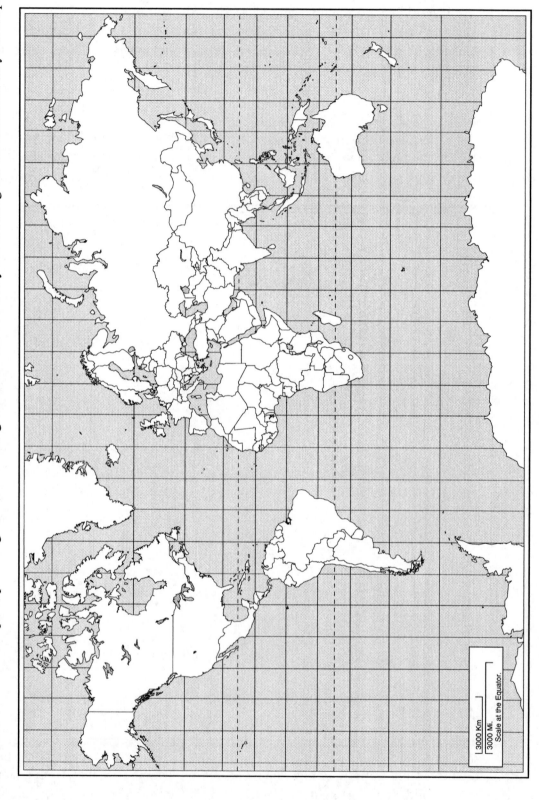

3000 Km
3000 Mi.
Scale at the Equator.

Legends in Your Own Mind

Although information about geological occurrences, such as earthquakes, was developing in the 19th century, it was not until the late 1960's that scientists were able to explain their causes. Long ago, people who lived in areas where earthquakes took place often made up stories to explain them.

Activity

Read the following examples of earthquake legends. Imagine that you lived long ago in a specific place in the world, and that you have no knowledge of the scientific explanations of earthquakes. Research to find out about the natural features, climate, and people of that region as they might have existed a long time ago. Then, use the examples to help you to write your own legend on page 70, explaining the reasons for earthquakes in the area you chose.

Earthquake Legend Examples

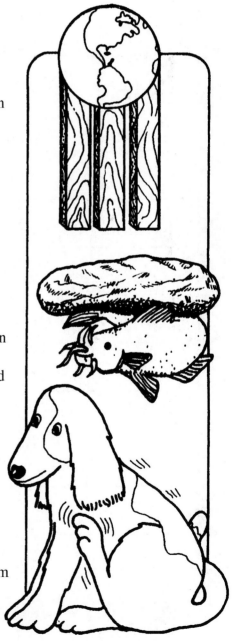

Columbia

When the earth was first made, it rested firmly on three large beams of wood. One day, the god Chibchacum decided that it would be fun to see the plain of Bogata underwater. He flooded the land, and for his punishment he was forced to carry the world on his shoulders. When he gets angry, he stomps his foot, shaking the earth.

Greece

According to the Greek philosopher Aristotle, strong winds are trapped and held in underground caverns. Earthquakes are caused by the wind's struggle to escape.

Japan

A huge catfish is curled up under the ocean, with the island of Japan resting on his back. A demigod (part god, part human) holds a heavy stone over the catfish to keep it still. Sometimes the demigod gets tired and looks away, the catfish moves, and Japan shakes.

Mexico

When El Diablo, the devil, wants to stir up trouble for people on earth, he makes giant rips in the ground from inside the earth.

Siberia

The earth rides on a sled driven by a god named Tuli and pulled through the heavens by dogs. The dogs have fleas which make them stop to scratch, causing the earth to shake.

Legends in Your Own Mind *(cont.)*

_____
title

_____

_____

_____

_____

_____

_____

_____

_____

_____

_____

_____

Geological Time Periods

Research to find information about the geological time periods listed below. Fill in the blank next to each time period with the letter that matches the correct time span.

Time Period		**Time Span**
1. Cambrian	_____	a. 10,000 – 2 million years ago
2. Cretaceous	_____	b. 1.5 million – 65 million years ago
3. Devonian	_____	c. 65 million – 135 million years ago
4. Jurassic	_____	d. 135 million – 192 million years ago
5. Mississippian	_____	e. 192 million – 225 million years ago
6. Ordovician	_____	f. 225 million – 280 million years ago
7. Pennsylvanian	_____	g. 280 million – 320 million years ago
8. Permian	_____	h. 320 million – 345 million years ago
9. Quaternary	_____	i. 345 million – 395 million years ago
10. Silurian	_____	j. 395 million – 435 million years ago
11. Tertiary	_____	k. 435 million – 500 million years ago
12. Triassic	_____	l. 500 million – 570 million years ago

Extension

Make a time line using the time period information (Time Span and Time Period name) in the correct areas of the time line. Use the time line to record geological information you discover.

Rocks Tell Tales — How Old Is It?

Geologists are able to tell, by laboratory tests, how long ago a rock was formed. Fossils are the same age as the rock in which they are found. It takes thousands and thousands of years for rocks to be formed. The oldest rocks are thought to be at least 4 ½ billion years old.

Humans also become fossils, as do plants and animals. In 79 A.D., the volcano Vesuvius erupted, burying people and buildings instantly. When archaeologists began digging in the ruins of Pompeii in 1860, Giuseppe Fiorelli produced plaster casts of human victims whose bodies had been encased in lava but left hollow shells after their bodies decayed. The shells were filled with plaster, allowed to harden, and then the pumice and ash that were part of the molds were chipped away. Lifelike forms of the victims were created in the positions in which they had encountered death.

In 1924, an almost complete skull of a child was found among limestone rocks in a cave in South Africa. This child was more than a million years old.

In 1974, an excavation for a housing development near the Black Hills of South Dakota uncovered fossilized bones of Columbian mammoths trapped 26,000 years ago.

In 1974, a bone protruding from the eroded slope of a gully was discovered in north-central Ethiopia. It had been buried under layers of sediment and volcanic ash. A flash flood eroded the rock layers away from this bone. Radioisotopic dating placed the age of these bones at about 3 million years ago. Scientists called the bone structure "Lucy."

In 1985, the foundation of an office building was being excavated in Austin, Texas. Fossils of mastodons were discovered. Radio-carbon dating of the strata above and below the bones deemed their age to be 15,000 years old.

Activity

Using the geological periods from page 71, answer the following questions.

1. In what period did the volcano, Vesuvius, eruption bury the city and people of Pompeii?

   _____

2. In what period did the South African child, discovered in 1924, exist?

   _____

3. From what geological time period was "Lucy"?

   _____

Extension: See if you can find additional information from the geological time periods to include on the time line. (See extension activity on page 71.) Write the responses from the questions above into the time line.

Art Projects

Rock Star Band

Collect some rocks of various shapes and sizes. Decorate them to look like rock musicians. Glue fake hair, eyes, etc. on them. Out of cardboard, aluminum foil, or other material you decide to use, make replicas of musical instruments for your "rock stars" to play. Use a small wooden box or drawer as a stage on which to display your "rock stars."

Build a Castle

Gather a large assortment of small rocks or stones. Use them to build a house, or castle, or perhaps an assortment of buildings. On a suitable sized board or cardboard, draw an outline of the project you wish to build. Place glue along part of the outline. Begin placing some of your larger rocks in the glue. Make sure your rocks are as clean as possible. Fill in the space between the big rocks with smaller stones. Continue to add more along the outline as you did the first section. When you have completed your entire outline, allow this layer to dry before adding the next layer. Use thick cardboard or wood for frames for doors and windows.

Montage

Collect pictures of mountains, volcanoes, rocks, gems, minerals, etc. Cut them out of newspapers and magazines. Glue or paste them to large letters you've cut out of construction paper, spelling GEOLOGY. Attach the letters to butcher paper or an old sheet to use as a banner to display in your room.

"Grand" Sand Paintings

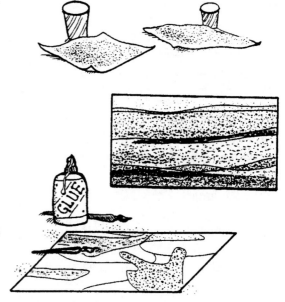

Materials: pencils; white construction paper; sand; paper cups; liquid food coloring; water; plastic spoons; paper towels; liquid white glue; small paintbrushes

Note: Pre-dye sand a few days before this activity by filling paper cups half-full with sand. Add water to the cup until the sand is completely covered. Add drops of one color of food coloring per cup (the more drops, the more vibrant the color). Stir the sand, water, and food dye using a spoon. Let it set for 20 minutes. Pour off as much liquid as possible without pouring out the sand. Spread drained sand on paper towels and let the sand dry completely. For variety, try different color combinations.

Directions: Draw lines with pencil across the white construction paper. Squirt a small amount of glue in one area between the lines. Spread the glue around with a paintbrush. Sprinkle one color of dyed sand in that area. Shake off the excess. Repeat the procedure with other sands to create colorful layers. Set the painting aside to dry. Display the sand paintings around one or more large pictures of the Grand Canyon, the Painted Desert, or other multi-colored sandstone scenes.

Geology Careers

Read about each of the occupations listed. Research one from the list. Tell why you might choose that particular occupation as a career. Describe the education and skills you might need, how you would achieve them, the duties involved, and any goals you have.

Geologists study the ways in which the parts of the earth fit together. They also examine parts of the earth to see what they are made of. They often explore and map different landforms, such as mountains and valleys. Some of their projects involve drilling through layers of the earth's crust to find out what kinds of rocks lie beneath the surface. Geologists identify rocks, minerals, fossil fuels, and precious stones such as diamonds. Trained geologists are employed by companies that use raw materials that come from the ground. Oil, coal, metals, gems, sulphur, asbestos, borax, and salt are some of the things geologists are hired to investigate. They calculate the best places to build dams, highways, tunnels, and skyscrapers. Individual states and the federal government need geologists to make geological surveys and investigate specific areas.

Volcanologists deal with volcanoes, especially those that are active or might become active. They monitor volcanoes with round-the-clock observation. They observe, take, and interpret measurements of changes in the behavior of an active volcano between and during eruptions. Monitoring volcanic activity provides some of the information needed to predict a volcano's future behavior.

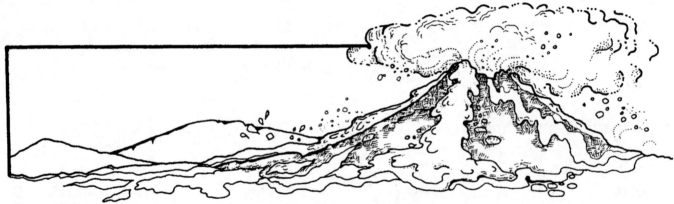

Seismologists are scientists who study earthquakes and the plate movements producing them. Using satellite observations and modern "tiltmeters" based on laser beams, they can sometimes detect tiny movements of the crust that indicate an earthquake is building up. The more information they gather, the greater their accuracy in predicting quakes so that warnings will be given in time to allow people to leave the area.

Hydrologists collect information about the earth's present and future water supplies. They study the ground and soil to learn whether water will stay in the soil or drain away. To find water sources, they study how the earth's crust is formed in a region.

Crystallographers pass x-rays through minerals, and by many other scientific tests, they can deduce the pattern of molecules inside the crystal, and tell you which elements are present and how they're combined.

Related occupations include: **mineralogist, paleontologist, glaciologist, oceanographer,** and **microscopist.**

Campfire Cooking

If you have an opportunity to go camping with your family (or perhaps your class can go on an outing), try cooking a meal over an open campfire, as Brighty experienced in *Brighty of the Grand Canyon.*

When cooking over an open fire, you must first prepare something to contain your fire source, if one isn't available. Gather various sizes of rocks to make a fire ring. Also clear the area, beyond the ring, of dried grass, leaves, and twigs to eliminate sparks starting a fire outside your ring. A cooking fire is not the same as a bonfire. A cooking fire should have coals, not a roaring fire! If you place a flat rock in the center of your ring, on a slight mound, the heat from the fire will heat the rock. The coals will keep it hot. You can put a cast iron griddle, pan, or pot on the rock.

Use a Dutch oven. Just like your oven at home, your Dutch oven needs heat all around it to cook evenly. Some Dutch ovens have indented covers to hold coals. Burying the oven allows the dirt or sand to hold the heat, which is important for long baking of foods such as beans. You can bake biscuits, corn bread, or even cake, in a Dutch oven. It takes a lot of practice to learn how to regulate the heat so you don't burn or undercook your food.

Brighty dined on frijoles. ("Frijole" is Spanish for "bean.") Here is a recipe for "Campfire Beans" that can be prepared over the course of a day.

Campfire Beans

Note: This activity requires adult supervision.

Directions

1. Soak 11/2 cups (about 350 mL) of dried beans in a Dutch oven (cast iron covered kettle). Cover them with water. Bring them to a boil, then simmer slowly for 1/2 hour or more, until tender. Drain the beans but save the water.

2. Add (more or less according to taste): 1/4 cup (60 mL) chopped onion; 2 tablespoons (30 mL) molasses or honey; 3 tablespoons (45 mL) catsup; 1 tablespoon (15 mL) dry mustard; 1 teaspoon (5 mL) salt; 1/2 cup (118 mL) boiling bean water; 1/4 pound (about 110 g) of sliced salt pork or bacon.

3. Have ready at least 2 to 3 quarts (1.9 L to 2.85 L) of hot coals. Dig a hole deep enough and wide enough to hold a Dutch oven, allowing about 4 extra inches (10 cm) to the depth of the hole for the coals. Put half of the coals in the bottom of the hole. Place the covered kettle of beans in the hole. Cover the lid with a large piece of foil to keep out dirt. Put the rest of the coals on top. Fill in the rest of the hole with dirt and put at least 3 inches (8 cm) of dirt or sand on top of the kettle. Don't dig in to peek for at least 4 hours. This recipe makes about 4 servings.

   You may not be able to dine on lion steaks, as Teddy Roosevelt did, but how about some hamburgers and hot dogs? Whatever you prepare, remember the fire safety rules and have a safe, enjoyable experience.

Geology Exhibition

Set aside a day at the end of the thematic unit to have a Geology Exhibition. Invite another class, parents and relatives, senior citizen groups, etc., to view the many projects accomplished while studying the *Geology* thematic unit.

- Set up booths to display the science projects: Magnetic Fields, Rock Collections, Erosion Experiment, and any additional geology projects. Invite visitors to ask questions. Have students demonstrate the projects and be ready to answer any questions.

- Display exceptional math papers, art projects, social studies, writing, and language arts activities in a prominent place in the classroom.

- Enlarge social studies maps to display volcanoes throughout the world and mines in the U.S.

- Display and/or demonstrate the model volcanoes to explain volcanic eruptions and some rock formations.

- Invite an area geologist as a guest speaker. Encourage the speaker to present a visual presentation as part of the program. Encourage the community to be present. By being better informed about the geological past, we might be able to conserve the area landscape in the future.

- Simulate the effects of weathering on sandstone by conducting these two experiments for the Geology Exhibition.

Experiment A

1. Weigh a piece of dry sandstone.

2. Place it in a container similar in size.

3. Cover the sandstone with water that has been weighed in advance.

4. Let the sandstone soak overnight.

5. After 24 hours, compare the weights of dry and wet sandstone.

6. Decide which is easier to break, wet sandstone or dry sandstone. Entertain suggestions about why one is easier to break than the other.

Experiment B

1. After soaking sandstone in water overnight, place a sample in the freezer for 24 hours along with a dry piece of sandstone.

2. After removal, record the effects of freezing water on the rock. Compare it to the dry, frozen sandstone.

3. Use the experiment results to draw conclusions about the effects of freezing water on the earth's rocks.

Have students demonstrate and/or display other experiments from the unit, or other geology experiments they find that relate to the unit.

Bulletin Board Ideas

Volcanoes

- Prepare a large volcano diagram for the center of a bulletin board. Label the various parts. Display appropriate papers and projects about volcanoes suggested in the unit.

- Enlarge the world map (page 68). Include the information required in the exercise. Have students prepare note cards with additional information about the features on the map.

We've Got a Gem of an Idea!

Enlarge the miner and gem pictures from page 78, and place them on a bulletin board. Display student papers from the Daily Writing Topics (pages 42-43) and other student writing examples suggested throughout the unit. Here are some title suggestions for the bulletin board: *The Magic School Bus Journeys Into Our Imaginations; We've Got a Gem of an Idea!*

Birthstones

Display the following information in the center of a bulletin board area:

Birthstones	
January—Garnet	**July**—Ruby
February—Amethyst	**August**—Peridot or Sardonyx
March—Aquamarine	**September**—Sapphire
April—Diamond or Bloodstone	**October**—Opal or Tourmaline
May—Emerald	**November**—Topaz
June—Pearl, Alexandrite, or Moonstone	**December**—Turquoise or Zircon

If possible, provide pictures for each, or illustrate a large gem in the middle of the bulletin board with information on birthstones surrounding it. Have students display their birthstone stories (page 56) next to the appropriate month.

Our Reports Are In Great Shape!

Display student-created shape books. (See page 45 for directions.) Shape books can be written and displayed for any number of topics in this unit. For example, shape books resembling crystals can be made for the students' writing about gems or crystals.

Enjoy a "Wheel" Good Book

Display the wheel books students have made. (See pages 45, 48, and 49.) Encourage students to create wheel books displaying information from a variety of topics in the unit.

Geology Journeys

Make a bar graph to show the extra material read by each student from the collection of books, magazines, and pamphlets assembled and/or used for research in this thematic unit. Include resource materials from the school or public library. Total the number of items from each resource (magazine, nonfiction book, fiction book, pamphlet, etc.) that were collectively used by the students. Represent these totals on the graph.

Award/Clip Art

Congratulations!

Way to go, _____ !

(student)

You've dug around
and found a treasure
of information.

What a splendid
report!

_____
(date)

_____
(teacher)

Answer Key

Page 10
A=14, B=10, C=4, D=1, E=7, F=2, G=13, H=6, I=12, J=8, K=3, L=5, M=9, N=11

Page 11
1=T, 2=F, 3=T, 4=T, 5=F, 6=F, 7=F, 8=T, 9=T, 10=F, 11=F, 12=F, 13=F, 14=T

Page 22
A=312, B=638, C=12, D=201, E=176, F=111, G=21, H=49, I=213, J=90, K=13, L=92, M=75, N=96, O=14, P=444, Q=156, R=760, S=32, T=499, U=186, V=626, W=23, X=91, Y=820, Z=926

1. caldera, 2. seismometer, 3. volcanology, 4. eruptions, 5. magma, 6. planets, 7. explosive, 8. pyroclastic, 9. mudflows, 10. pumice

Page 28
A=6; B=8; C=9; D=3; E=5; F=7; G=9; H=8

Page 29

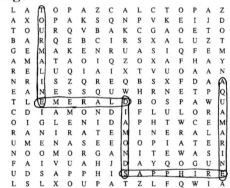

Page 35
1. crevice, 2. river, 3. meadow, 4. abyss, 5. rift, 6. mesa, 7. canyon, 8. plateau, 9. creek, 10. cliff, 11. parapet, 12. cave, 13. mountain, 14. forest

Page 39
Erosion experiment: The soil should be carried away the farthest, the sand next, then pebbles, and lastly the large stones.

Page 51

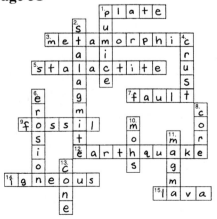

Page 52

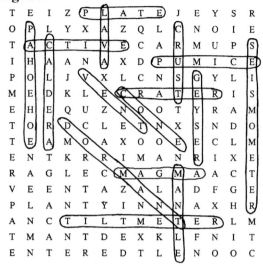

Page 57
1. 1300; 2. 170; 3. 100; 4. 1783; 5. 9; 6. 597; 7. 15; 8. 95; 9. 5

Page 58
diamond = 52 (10)   corundum = 40 (9)
talc = 6 (1)   feldspar = 31 (6)
quartz = 36 (7)   calcite= 22 (3)
gypsum = 21 (2)   topaz = 38 (8)
fluorite = 29 (4)   apatite = 30 (5)

Page 59
1. compounds, 2. ores, 3. fool's gold, 4. arsenic, 5. oxides, 6. carbonates, 7. Nitrates, 8. Gypsum

Page 66
1. limestone, 2. limestone, 3. shale, 4. sandstone,   5. shale, 6. shale, 7. granite

Page 71
1=l, 2=c, 3=i, 4=d, 5=h, 6=k, 7=g, 8=f, 9=a, 10=j, 11=b, 12=e

Page 72
1. Quaternary, 2. Quaternary, 3. Tertiary

Bibliography

Arem, Dr. Joel E. *Discover Rocks & Minerals.* (Publications International, Ltd., 1991)

Asimov, Isaac. *Asimov's Biographical Encyclopedia of Science and Technology,* 2nd Revised Ed. (Doubleday & Company, 1982)

Beach, James Caleb. *Theodore Roosevelt, Man of Action.* (Garrard Press, 1960)

Berger, Melvin. *Disastrous Volcanoes.* (Franklin Watts, 1981)

Cavanah, Frances. *Adventure in Courage—The Story of Theodore Roosevelt.* (E.M. Hale & Company, 1961)

Cole, Joanna. *The Magic School Bus Inside the Earth.* (Scholastic, Inc. 1987)

Fishbein, Semour L. *Grand Canyon Country: Its Majesty and Its Lore.* (National Geographic Society: Book Division, 1991)

Harlow, Alvin F. *Theodore Roosevelt—Strenuous American.* (Julian Messner, Inc. 1962)

Henry, Marguerite. *Black Gold.* (Macmillan, 1957)

    Born to Trot. (Macmillan, 1950)

    Brighty of the Grand Canyon. (Scholastic, Inc. 1967)

    Justin Morgan Had a Horse. (Macmillan, 1954)

    King of the Wind. (Macmillan, 1948)

    Misty of Chincoteague. (Macmillan, 1947)

    Sea Star: Orphan of Chincoteague. (Macmillan, 1949)

    Stormy: Misty's Foal. (Macmillan, 1963)

    White Stallion of Lipizza. (Macmillan, 1979)

Hussey, Lois J. & Pessino, Catherine. *Collecting Small Fossils.* (Thomas Y. Crowell Company, 1970)

Jeanes, Charlotte & Muench, Joyce Rockwood. *Grand Canyon Hike.* (Follet, 1962)

Judson, Clara Ingram. *Theodore Roosevelt—Fighting Patriot.* (Follet, 1953)

Marcus, Elizabeth. *The Question & Answer Book—Rocks & Minerals.* (Troll Associates, 1983)

Roberts, Royston M. *Serendipity—Accidental Discoveries in Science.* (Wiley Science Editions—John Wiley & Sons, Inc., 1989)

Simon, Seymour. *Volcanoes.* (Morrow Jr. Books, 1988)

Van Rose, Susanna. *Eyewitness Books: Volcano and Earthquake.* (Alfred A, Knopf, 1992)

Waldman, Carl. *Encyclopedia of Native American Tribes.* (Facts on File Publications, 1988)

Wood, Jenny. *Wonderworks of Nature: Icebergs—Titans of the Oceans.* (Gareth Stevens, 1991)

Wood, Jenny. *Wonderworks of Nature: Volcanoes—Fire From Below.* (Gareth Stevens, 1991)